THE
ART
OF
INVENTION

A GUIDE
TO THE
WORLD'S
WEIRDEST PATENTS

BY UWE DIEGEL

ABOUT UWE DIEGEL

Uwe Diegel was born in New Zealand in 1965. He then moved from country to country, every four years, living in Mobile Alabama, Chicoutimi Quebec, and then arriving in South Africa at the age of 16. He was a classical concert pianist until the age of 26. Following a dramatic accident, he partially lost the use of his right arm and recycled himself as a medical researcher and in industrial design.

Over the years, he has been an ice cream manufacturer, a restaurant owner, a manufacturer of medical devices, an expert in antique silverware and an artist. He is today a leading authority in the management of chronic diseases and a manufacturer of medical devices.

He is the published author of over 20 books on various medical subjects and is today CEO of HealthWorks (www.medactiv.com) and Lifeina (www.lifeina.com), both companies manufacturing medical devices.

He is also the proud owner of one of the world's largest collections of antique blood pressure devices and his website (www.bloodpressurehistory.com) is a reference in this field.

As an artist, his work is profoundly irreverent, possibly irrelevant, but always fun. Deeply anti-religious, deeply anti-political, deeply anti-vegan, deeply anti-brocoli, deeply anti-anything-he-doesn't-like, he creates devices, products, toys, really weird stuff based on his spur of the moment moods and inspiration. Discover his works on www.desirinfernal.com.

THE INFERNAL DESIRE MACHINES
OF UWE DIEGEL
"BITE THE PILLOW, I'M GOING IN DRY"
Discover

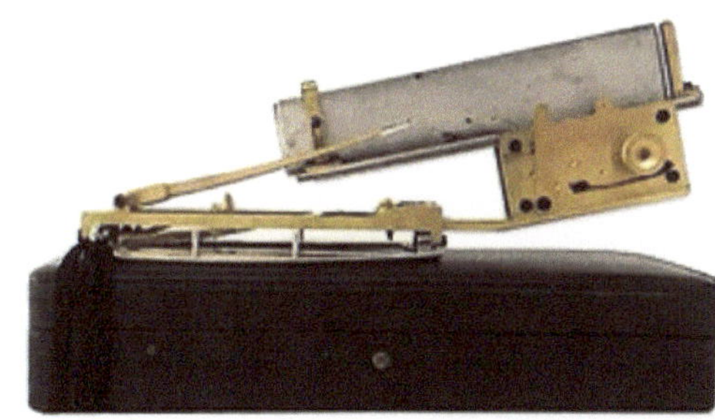
BLOOD PRESSURE HISTORY

"IT IS ONLY BY LOOKING AT THE PAST THAT
WE CAN UNDERSTAND THE FUTURE"

Uwe DIEGEL

lifeina

Travel the world

Be free

Live your life

5D
Keeps insulin cool
for 5 days

medactiv
transforming lives

The art of invention and design

Everything is invented and designed, one way or another. Some objects are designed well, while others are not; some are designed pretentiously, others unassumingly; some are designed to optimize materials and techniques, while others are wasteful. While some objects naturally attract our attention for their extraordinary character and desirability - an eccentric and expensive pair of sneakers, for instance, or a gleaming sports car - many others are so apparently ordinary as to go unnoticed. Every day we use dozens of them, from elastic bands to Band-Aids, erasers, and mascara wands. If they work well, chances are we won't pay them much attention. However, in spite of their modest price and demure presence, some of these things are true masterpieces of the art of design and deserve our unconditional admiration.

Are all inventions essential or useful?

Space has its urban legends of course, and the **Million Dollar Space Pen** is one of the more enduring ones. It is neither as outlandish nor as unbelievable as the story about faking the Moon landings, and even though it seems more credible than a massive government conspiracy, it is probable that fewer people have heard it.

The story goes like this: in the 1960s, NASA astronauts discovered that their pens did not work in zero gravity. So like good engineers, they went to work and designed a wonder, million dollar pen. It worked upside down. It worked in vacuum. It worked in zero gravity. It even worked underwater! **And it only cost a million dollars!**

At the same time, the Russians were ramping up their efforts to conquer space before the Americans, and they also realized that their normal pens did not work in space…

So the crafty Russians used a pencil…

Every now and then, people have ideas. Some of them are *"Eureka"* moments, a sudden illumination. A flash of imagination that drives progress forward. And often a patent is needed... A patent is defined as *"a government authority or licence conferring a right or title for a set period, especially the sole right to exclude others from making, using, or selling an invention"*.

Basically, in layman's terms, *"**I have to protect this before someone else has the idea and steals it from me !!!**"*.

Anything, from glasses for chickens, dog umbrellas, breast-shaped pillows to rooster-shaped airplanes can be patented, and has been. Here is a collection of some of the funniest, most ridiculous or even absurd patents deposed since the 31st of July 1790, when Samuel Hopkins was issued the world's first patent for a process of making potash, an ingredient used in fertilizer.

Improvement in Combined Plow and Gun

French, C. M., Fancher W. H., *Combined Plow and Guns*, UNITED STATES PATENT OFFICE Patent No. 35,600, June 17, 1862.

The object of our invention is to produce a plow equal, if not superior, in point of strength and lightness to that implement as ordinarily made, and at the same time to combine in its construction the elements of light ordnance, so that when the occasion offers it may do valuable service in the capacity of both implements.

This combination enables those in agricultural pursuits to have at hand an efficient weapon of defense at a very slight expense.

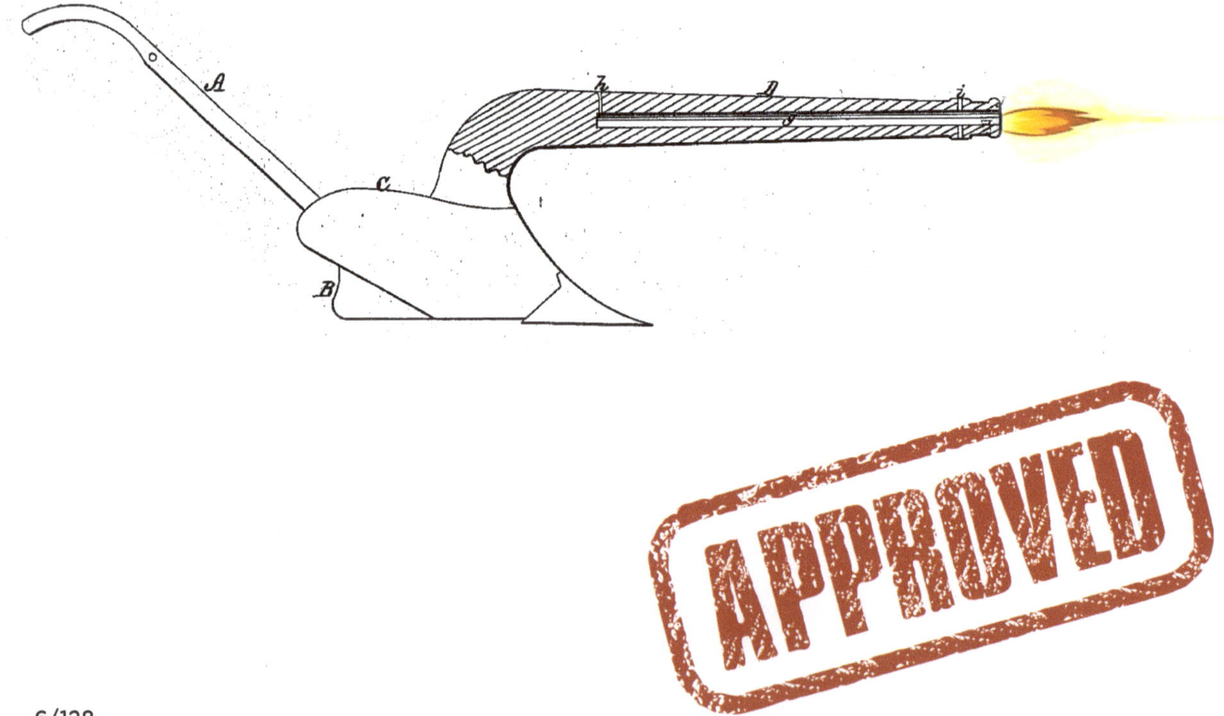

Improved Rocking-Chair

Singer, Charles, *Improved Rocking-Chair*, UNITED STATES PATENT OFFICE Patent No. 92,379, July 06, 1869.

This invention relates to improvements in the construction of rocking-chairs, with air-blowing attachments, having for its object to provide a stand or base for the support of a bellows, with tracks or rails, on which the rockers, which are fixed close to the seat, may work, instead of oil the floor; also, to provide an arrangement whereby the parts may be readily detached for storage or packing in compact form; and also an improved arrangement of parts, whereby the bellows is operated.

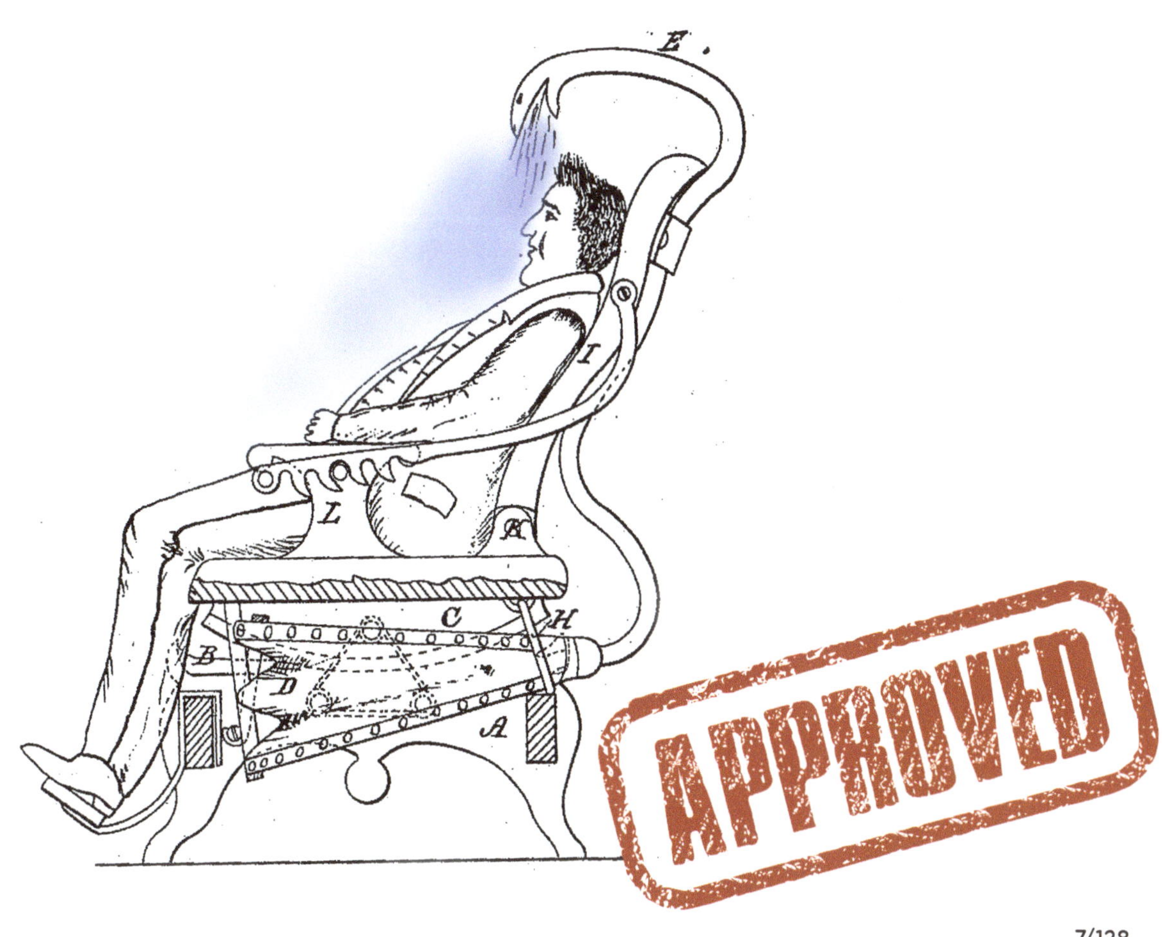

Improved Burglar Trap

Carr, W., *Improved Burglar Trap*, UNITED STATES PATENT OFFICE Patent No. 77,582, May 5, 1868.

This invention relates to a trap which is to be located in a cellar or basement under a store or office, and the apparatus is provided with doors, which are on a level with the floor of the store, the doors being arranged in such a manner as to open, the instant the burglar steps on them, and deposit him in the trap.

The apparatus is so arranged that the burglar rests upon a false bottom, which is connected to the trapdoors with rods or chains, by which means the weight of the occupant serves to keep the doors closed, and thus, prevents his escape.

The principal part of the trap consists of a chamber, A, which is placed beneath the ground-floor of a store, and this chamber is divided in three parts by means of the vertical partitions B B', the central part, A, of the chamber being for the retention of the burglar, while the other two, A, A', contain the devices for operating the doors.

Improved Burglar Trap

Carr, W., *Improved Burglar Trap*, UNITED STATES PATENT OFFICE Patent No. 77,582, May 5, 1868.

ILLUSTRATION

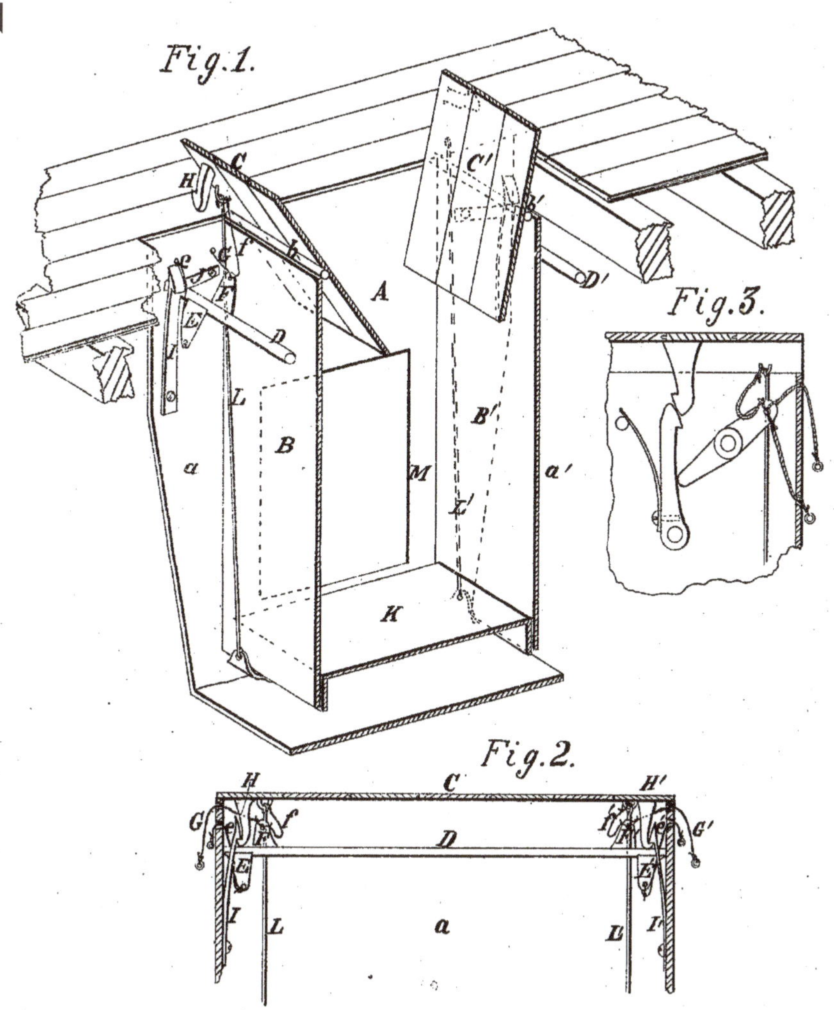

Figure 1 is a vertical section, partially in perspective, of a burglar-trap embodying improvement.

Figure 2 is a transverse section, taken through the upper part of the trap.

Figure 3 represents a modification of the device for operating the trap-doors.

Moustache Guard

Gates, Virgil A., *Moustache Guard,* UNITED STATES PATENT Patent No. 176,175, Mar. 18, 1876.

Every gentleman who wears a moustache must have experienced the great inconvenience it causes in eating and drinking, especially in eating soups and other kinds of food of similar consistency. The object of this invention is to obviate this inconvenience by providing a simple device, easily applied and removed, for holding the moustache out of the way of the food or liquid while eating or drinking.

Cork Swimming Suit

Paschal, P., George, B. Nichols, Flood, Isaac, *Cork Swimming Suit*, UNITED STATES PATENT Patent No. 267,799, Nov. 21, 1882.

The object of this invention is to produce a swimming-garment which shall not interfere at all with the perfectly free motions of the body and limbs; which shall be buoyant and thus aid swimmers, especially feeble swimmers; which shall permit the perfectly-free circulation of the water in contact with the skin, and which shall so fit and envelop the body as to cause but slight resistance, and perhaps none at all to progress in the water, on account of its pliability and buoyancy.

This invention consists of a jacket or garment, which is substantially a netting of small strong cords and small pieces of cork, fitting like an ordinary knit undershirt or small-scale armor.

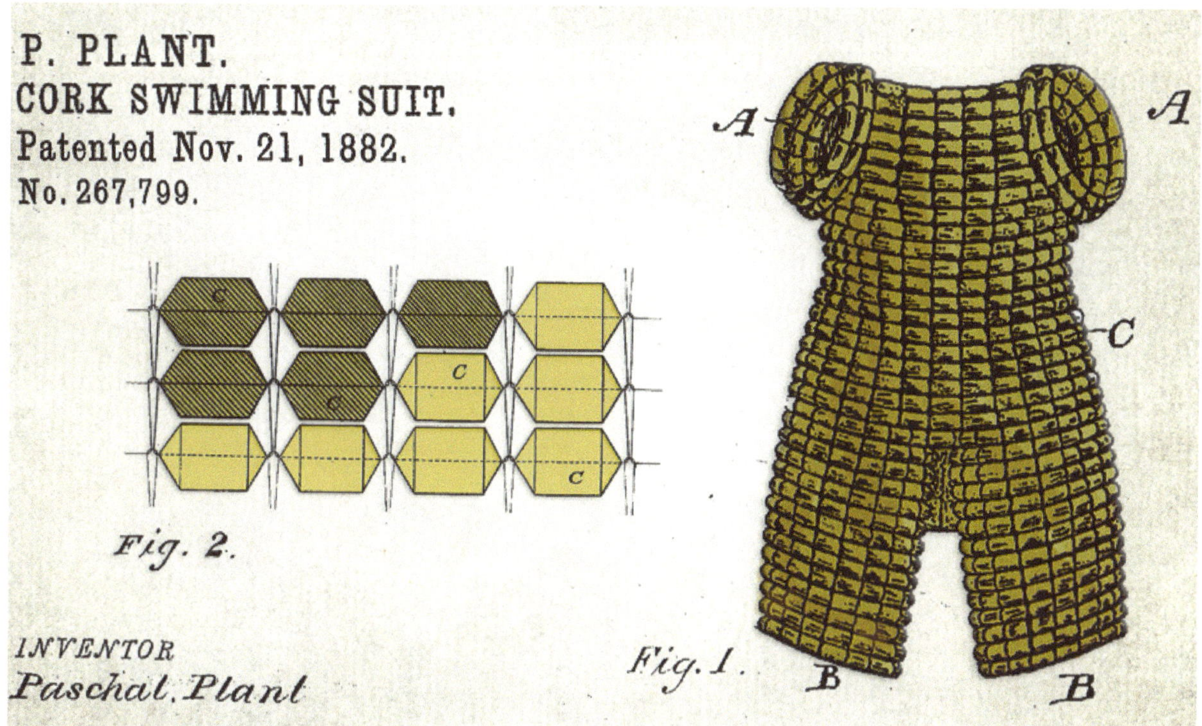

New and Improved Animal Trap

Williams, James A., *Animal Trap.* UNITED STATES PATENT OFFICE Patent No. 269,766, December 26, 1882.

Invention relates to improvements in animal-traps; and it consists in the combination of a suitable frame upon which a revolver or pistol is secured, a treadle which is secured to the front end of this frame, and a suitable spring and levers, by which the firearm is discharged when the animal steps upon the treadle, as will be more fully described hereinafter.

The object of my invention is to provide a means by which animals which burrow in the ground can be destroyed, and which trap will give an alarm each time that it goes off, so that it can be reset.

The animal, in coming out, steps upon the treadle and presses the treadle down, which releases the lever, when the spring immediately causes the lever to fly upward and the rod then forces back the trigger and causes the firearm to go off, killing the animal that is in front of it. This invention may also be used in connection with a door or window, so as to kill any person or thing opening the door or window to which it is attached.

New and Improved Animal Trap

Williams, James A., *Animal Trap.* UNITED STATES PATENT OFFICE Patent No. 269,766, December 26, 1882.

ILLUSTRATION

(A) represents a suitable board, from which rises the three standards (B), upon which the revolver or pistol (C) is supported in position. Pivoted to the middle standard is the lever (D), and fastened in any suitable manner to the front end of this lever is the rod (G), which extends backward and bears against the trigger of the fire-arm.

One Wheeled Vehicle

Loose, J. O., *One Wheeled Vehicle*, UNITED STATES PATENT Patent No. 325,548, Sept. 1, 1885.

This invention relates to a unicycle or one wheeled vehicle, without spokes, which will carry one or more persons, as well as a bicycle carries the passenger inside, and only one wheel touching the ground.

Device for Assisting Infirm Persons

Eustis, Allain, *Device for Assisting Infirm Persons*, UNITED STATES PATENT OFFICE Patent No. 535,825, March 19, 1895.

Invention has for its object to provide a device adapted to be used in assisting old or infirm persons in ascending steps, said device being provided with simple means for attachment to the assistant, whereby the application of power by the assistant is facilitated.

New and Improved Saluting Device

Boyle, James C., *Saluting Device.* UNITED STATES PATENT OFFICE Patent No. 556,248, March 10,1896.

This invention relates to a novel device for automatically effecting polite' salutations by the elevation and rotation of the hat on the head of the saluting party when said person bows to the person or persons sainted, the actuation of the hat being produced by mechanism therein and without the use of the hands in any manner.

The improvement is also available as a unique and attractive advertising medium, and may be employed for such a purpose. The invention consists in the novel construction, arrangement and combinations of 20 parts, as hereinafter described and claimed; Reference is to be had to the accompanying drawings, forming a part of this specification, in which similar characters of reference indicate corresponding parts in all the views.

New and Improved Saluting Device

Boyle, James C., *Saluting Device.* UNITED STATES PATENT OFFICE Patent No. 556,248, March 10, 1896.

ILLUSTRATION

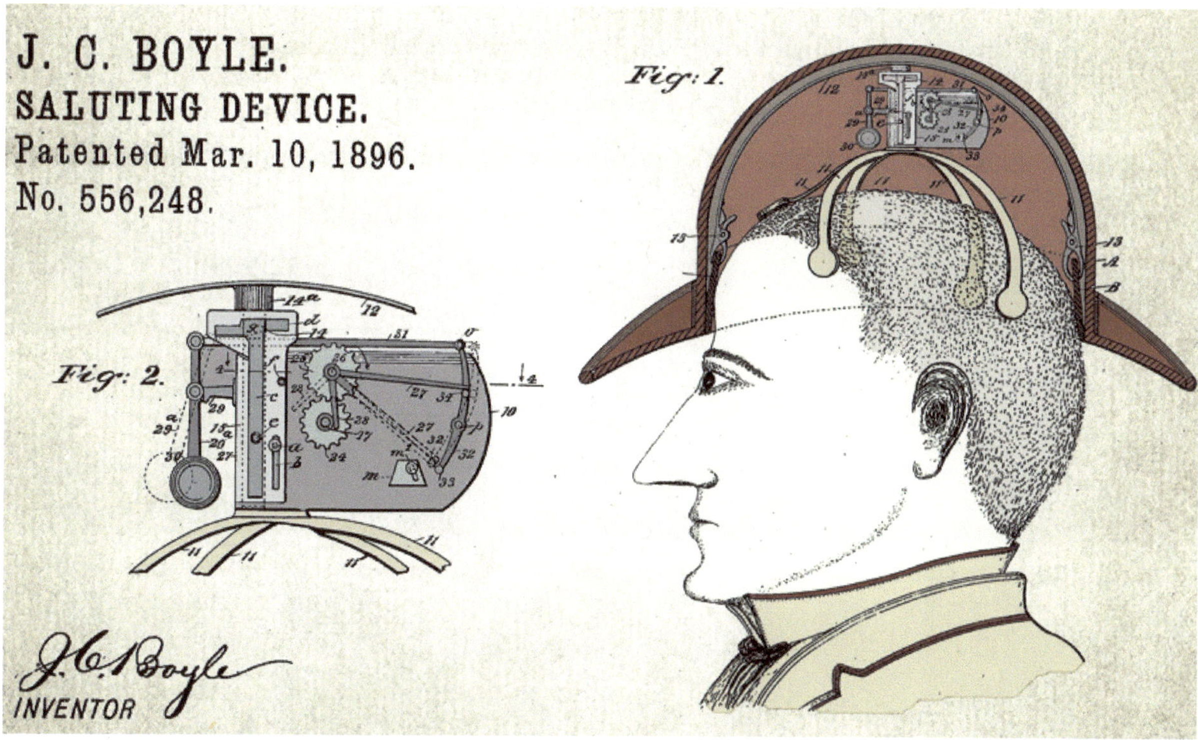

A mechanism held in a case removably clamped on the head of the wearer of the hat, while the hat is detachably secured to the working parts of the device that raise the hat, completely rotate it, and deposit it correctly on the head of the wearer every time said person bows his head and then assumes an erect posture, all parts of the novel device being completely inclosed in and concealed by the hat.

Rocking or Oscillating Bathtub

Hensel, O. A., *Rocking or Oscillating Bathtub*, UNITED STATES PATENT Patent No. 643,094, Feb. 6, 1900.

This invention relates to an improved rocking or oscillating bath-tub; and it consists of a tub mounted in journals formed in a suitable supporting-frame, a means for maintaining the equilibrium of the said tub, a means for locking the same in a horizontal position, a detachable covering fitted about the periphery of the tub, whereby the water contained therein is prevented from escaping, a means for confining the said covering in position, a means for connecting the two poles of an electromagnetic device to electrify the water in the tub, and a means formed in connection with the said covering whereby the occupant of the tub may reach the valves regulating and controlling the water-supply.

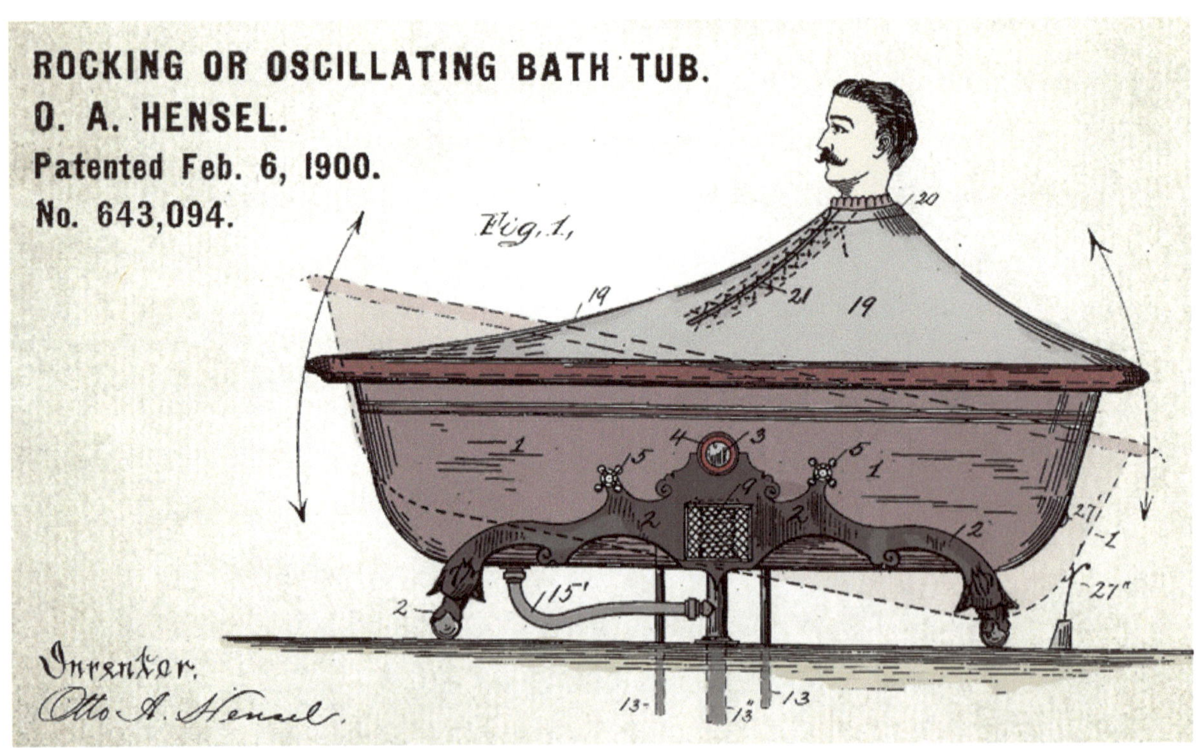

The Art of Invention 

Having a dream is easy. Everybody has dreams..

But realizing your dream is much more difficult. Changing an idea into a project, something that you can touch and feel, that you can show and be proud of, is an incredibly rewarding goal. This is why patents exist. Because creation takes time, perfection takes time.

At Lifeina, we know that the best inventions are driven by personnal needs.

Eye Protector for Chickens

Jackson, A. Jr., *Eye Protector for Chickens,* UNITED STATES PATENT Patent No. 730,918, June 16, 1903.

This invention relates to eye-protectors, and more particularly to eye-protectors designed for fowls, so that they may be protected from other fowls that might attempt to peck them, a further object of the invention being to provide a construction which may be easily and quickly applied and removed and which will not interfere with the sight of the fowl.

An additional object of the invention is to provide a construction which may be adjusted so that it will fit different-sized fowls.

In the drawings forming a portion of this specification, and in which like numerals of reference indicate similar parts in the several views, Figure 1 is a view showing the device attached to the head of a chicken. Fig. 2 is a perspective view of the device removed from the head of the chicken.

Eye Protector for Chickens

Jackson, A. Jr., *Eye Protector for Chickens*, UNITED STATES PATENT Patent No. 730,918, June 16, 1903.

Double Bicycle for Looping the Loop

Lange, K., *Double Bicycle for Looping the Loop*, UNITED STATES PATENT Patent No. 790,063, Mar. 24, 1904.

The present invention consists of a double bicycle for looping the loop for circus and other performances.

The object is to provide a cycle by means of which a mutilated loop may be traversed, the performer springing, with the wheel, off the end of the loop while head downward and running off onto a track leading out of the loop on the two upper wheels of the cycle head downward.

A cycle for looping a mutilated loop consisting of a frame having two wheels mounted on the lower part and two wheels mounted above the head of the rider, a saddle on the lower frame and a cushion on the upper frame to brace the rider.

A cycle for looping a mutilated loop, consisting of a frame, a pair of wheels mounted in the bottom portion of the frame and a pair of wheels mounted in the top portion of the frame, a saddle in the central portion of the frame, and a cushion in the top portion of the frame to brace the rider, said wheels being all in the same plane.

Double Bicycle for Looping the Loop

Lange, K., *Double Bicycle for Looping the Loop,* UNITED STATES PATENT Patent No. 790,063, Mar. 24, 1904.

Fire Escape Apparatus

Nigro, P., *Fire Escape Apparatus*, UNITED STATES PATENT OFFICE Patent No. 912,152, February 09, 1909.

Invention is an improvement in fire escapes, and consists in certain novel constructions and combinations of parts hereinafter described and claimed. The present embodiment of invention comprises a frame consisting of a central portion 1, adapted to be placed on the shoulders of the wearer and having a cut-away portion 2, for receiving the neck. The central portion 1 is provided at each side of the opening with strengthening ribs 3. The side sections 5 are hinged to the ends of the central sections, by a rule joint 6 as shown in Fig. 4. It will be observed that the side sections are curved longitudinally in the plane of the sections, and are provided adjacent to the commencement of the curved portion with loops 8 for engagement by tbe hands of the wearer as shown in Fig. 1.

The frame is provided with a covering of fabric material 9, and is secured to the body of the wearer by means of straps 10, which are riveted or otherwise secured to the central portion of the frame 1, as at 11, the straps crossing and being riveted together as at 12, the upper ends thereof being provided with buckles 13, and the lower ends with spaced openings 14 for engagement by the tongues of the buckles. A strap 15 is secured to the fabric material as at 16, the said strap being endless and forming a loop for engaging a belt 17.

Fire Escape Apparatus

Nigro, P., *Fire Escape Apparatus*, UNITED STATES PATENT OFFICE Patent No. 912,152, February 09, 1909.

ILLUSTRATION

A fire escape comprising a frame composed of a central section, and side sections hinged to the central section, means in connection with the hinges for preventing upward movement of the side sections with respect to the central section, the side sections being curved toward their outer ends, a covering of fabric material for the frame, straps connected with the central portion for securing said central portion to the shoulders, a loop connected with the fabric material, a belt engaged with the loop, and loops on the side sections for engagement by the hands of the wearer.

Scarecrow

Huffman, H., Peck, E. J., *Scarecrow*, UNITED STATES PATENT OFFICE Patent No. 1,167,502, January 11, 1916.

This invention relates to scare crows which are adapted to he used in a garden patch, field, or orchard for the purpose of scaring away intruding birds or animals which might eat or otherwise injure the crop.

A scare-crow comprising a standard, a rotatable arm adjustably mounted on the standard, wind vanes on one end of said arm, a flexible supporting element fixed to the other end of said arm, including a spring and a swivel, and a figure supported by said flexible element.

Prior to our invention, the scare crows ordinarily used were crude affairs, being generally home-made and not wholly satisfactory. One of the main objects of our invention is to provide a more efficient form of scare crow consisting of a figure formed to resemble a living animal in the posture of approaching its prey. The means of mounting this scare crow are so arranged that the action of the wind will give various motions to the figure which will simulate the lifelike movements of the animal. The figure is also provided with an audible alarm which will sound in accordance with the movements of the figure, so is to attract the attention of the intruding birds or animals.

Scarecrow

Huffman, H., Peck, E. J., *Scarecrow*, UNITED STATES PATENT OFFICE Patent No. 1,167,502, January 11, 1916.

ILLUSTRATION

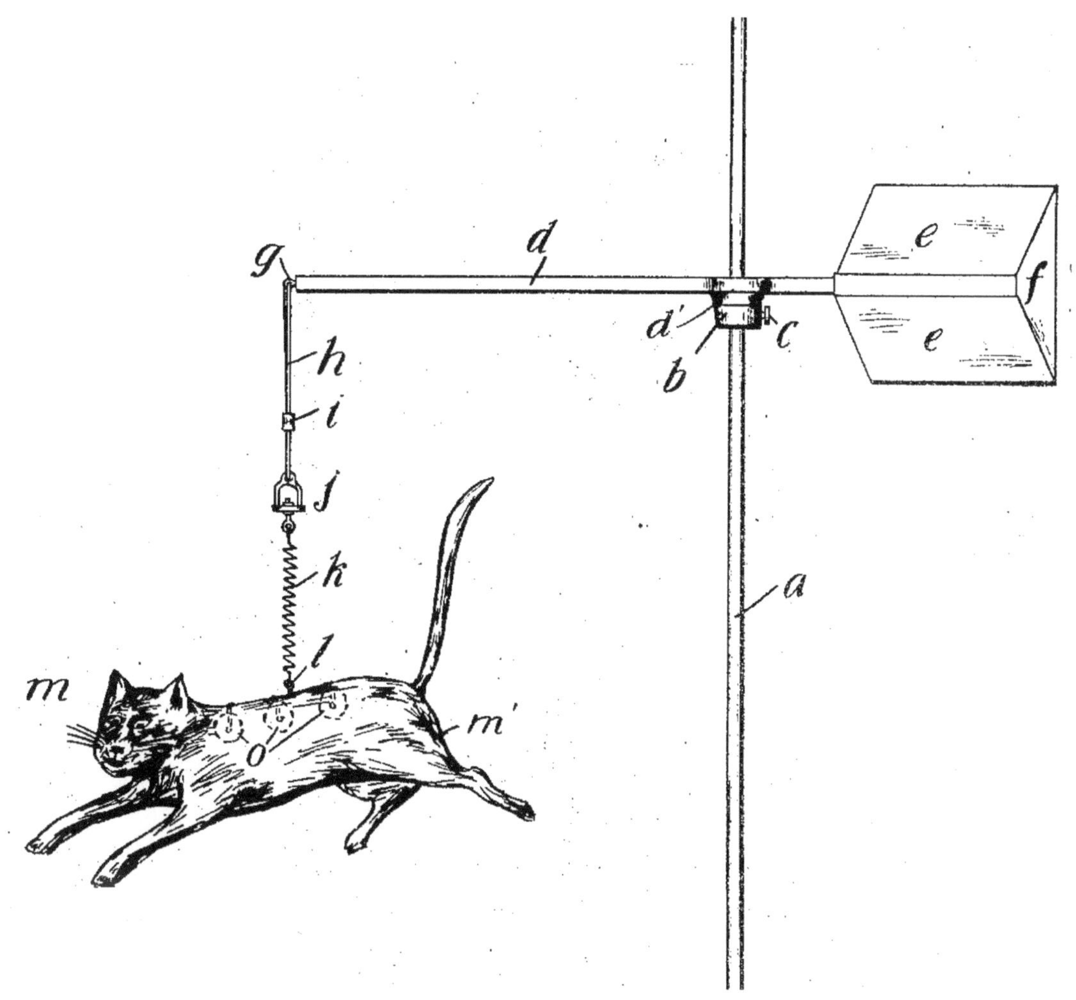

The scare crow proper consists of a figure (M) formed in this instance to represent a cat or other feline animal. The figure (M) is provided with a screw-eye (L) to which the lower end of the spring (K) is fastened, and so located that the figure is maintained in poised position.

Man-Catching Tank

Valinski, Stanley, *Man-Catching Tank*, UNITED STATES PATENT OFFICE Patent No.
1,392,095, September 27, 1921.

This invention relates to a man-catching tank and it is especially, although,
not necessarily, designed for use in banks for catching and holding
burglars or the like. The principal object of the invention is to provide a
device of this class embodying a portable motor-driven armored tank box
equipped with peep-holes, gun-openings and other conveniences, and
having on its exterior novel means for grabbing and holding the thief until
assistance arrives.

Exercising Device

Purdy, Charles, *Exercising Device*, UNITED STATES PATENT OFFICE Patent No. 1,466,559, August 28, 1923.

The present invention relates to new and to useful improvements in exercising devices, and it pertains more particularly to devices especially designed and constructed for exercising the teeth, gums and all other organs which under a natural diet would receive their exercise through the act of mastication.

It is the primary object of the invention to provide a device the use of which will supply the necessary exercise to the muscles of these several organs to keep said organs in a healthy state, and operate as a preventative agent and curative medicine in case of pyorrhea.

Aeroplane of Rooster Shape

Mateo, Angel, *Airplane of Rooster Shape*, UNITED STATES PATENT OFFICE Patent No. 1,810,182, June 16, 1931.

The invention proposes an aeroplane body simulating a rooster and having a pair of pivoted wings, a motor-driven traction propeller mounted on the front of said body, each of said wings being composed of inner and outer sections telescopically and slidably arranged in edge contacting relation, means for retracting the outer wing sections in lowered positions of the wings, means for projecting the outer wing sections in raised positions of the wings, and means for Raising and lowering said wings constituting flapping.

The aeroplane of roofer shape consists of an aeroplane body 10 simulating a rooster and having a pair of pivoted wings 11, a motor-driven traction propeller 12 mounted on the front of said body, each of said wings 11 being composed of inner sections 13 and outer sections 14 telescopically and slidably engaged in edge contacting relation, means for retracting the outer wing sections 14 in lowered positions of the wings, means for projecting the outer wing sections in raised positions of the wings, and means for raising and lowering said wings constituting flapping.

Aeroplane of Rooster Shape

Mateo, Angel, *Airplane of Rooster Shape*, UNITED STATES PATENT OFFICE Patent No. 1,810,182, June 16, 1931.

ILLUSTRATION

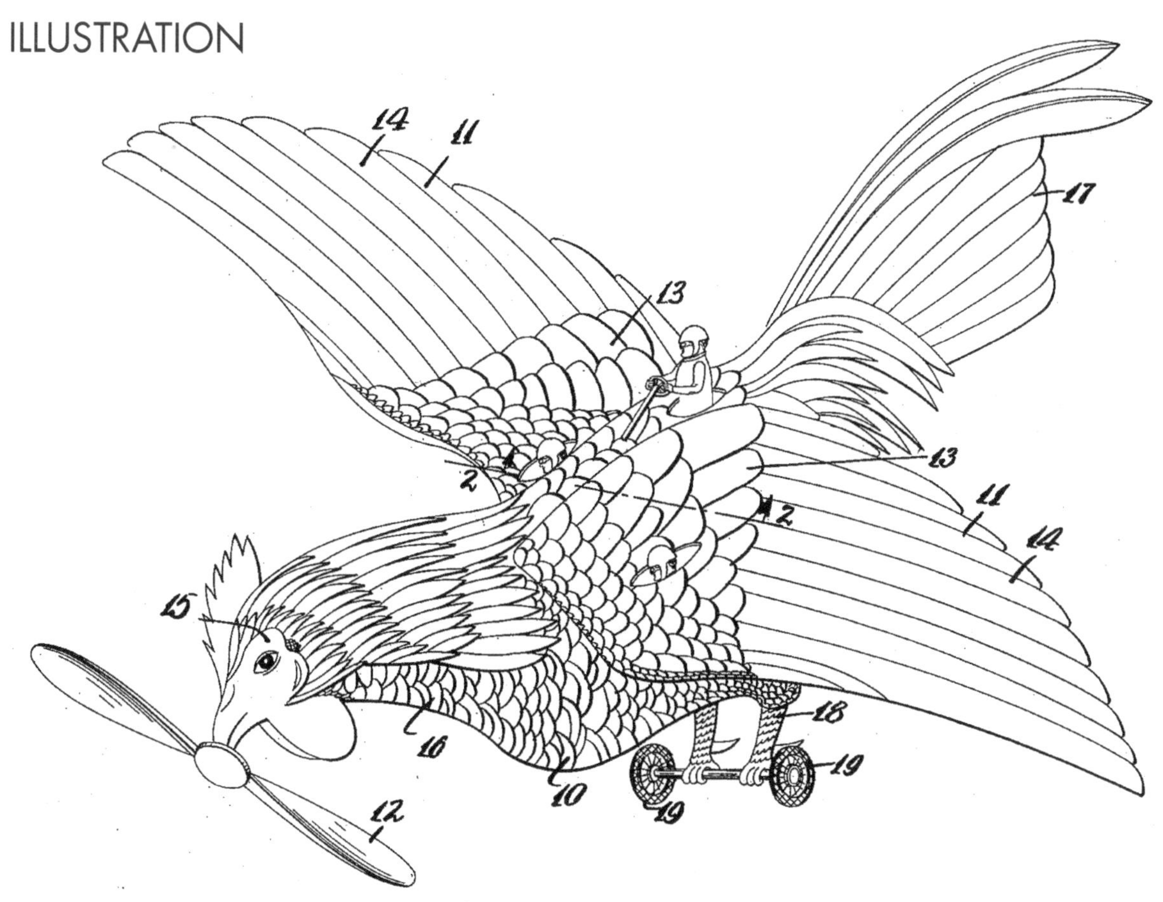

The aeroplane body 10 has a rooster head 15, neck 16, tail 17 and legs 18. The propeller 12 is mounted upon the bill of the head 15. The motor for driving the propeller is housed within the neck. Wheels 19 are mounted upon the legs 18 constituting the landing gear of the device. Each inner wing section 13 is pivotally mounted at its inner edge 20 on the said body 10 and is of hollow construction arranged so that the hollow communicates with the outer edge. The outer section 14 is slidably engaged in this hollow so as to extend therewith.

Cigarette Ring

Watson P. Aull, *Cigarette Ring*, UNITED STATES PATENT OFFICE Patent No. 2,109,609, March 01, 1938.

Objects of the invention are to provide a cigarette ring adapted to be worn upon the forefinger of the left hand and equipped with means to receive and hold a cigarette firmly at an upward angle across the back of the hand and separated from the hand a sufficient distance so that the burning cigarette will not cause discomfort; to provide means conveniently manipulative to release and eject the butt of the cigarette; to provide means for enclosing and covering the cigarette holding devices when they are not in use; and to provide the holding devices so that they will move to and retain a position in which the burning end of the cigarette is inclined outwardly away from the back of the hand.

Thumb Sucking Inhibitor

Orr, San Watterson and Orr, Eleanor Augusts, *Thumb Sucking Inhibitor*, UNITED STATES PATENT OFFICE Patent No. 2,442,176, May 25, 1948.

A thumb sucking inhibitor or novelty device in which the device is secured directly to the digit rather than being secured to the hand, or wrist or some similar place other than the digit.

By designing a key, separate and distinct from the inhibitor itself, it is possible to prevent an unauthorized removal of the inhibitor from the digit. An ornamental figure, which may be of a dog or the like, is secured to the cylindrical portion of the sheath so as to make an article too large to be swallowed by the child.

Boy's Toilet Trainer

Henoch, Rolph E. et all, *Boy's Toilet Trainer*, UNITED STATES PATENT OFFICE Patent No. 2,703,407, March 08, 1955.

The present invention relates to a boy's toilet trainer for the instruction and training of young boys to increase the sanitary cleanliness of bathrooms, and provides a simple inexpensive tool which may be applied to toilet bowls of standard size and construction.

A still further object of the invention is to provide a boy's toilet trainer of sufficient appeal to the young boys to make use of it prior to wetting their pants.

In accomplishing the above objects it has been found most satisfactory to provide a detachable mounted structure on which is mounted a swinging arm carrying a rotatable paddle member or spoon-like member. When the arm is moved into an operative position, it will provide a horizontally extended axis or pivot rod transverse to the fore-and-aft axis of the toilet bowl so that the stream of fluid will cause rotation of the paddle member.

Boy's Toilet Trainer

Henoch, Rolph E. et all, *Boy's Toilet Trainer*, UNITED STATES PATENT OFFICE Patent No. 2,703,407, March 08, 1955.

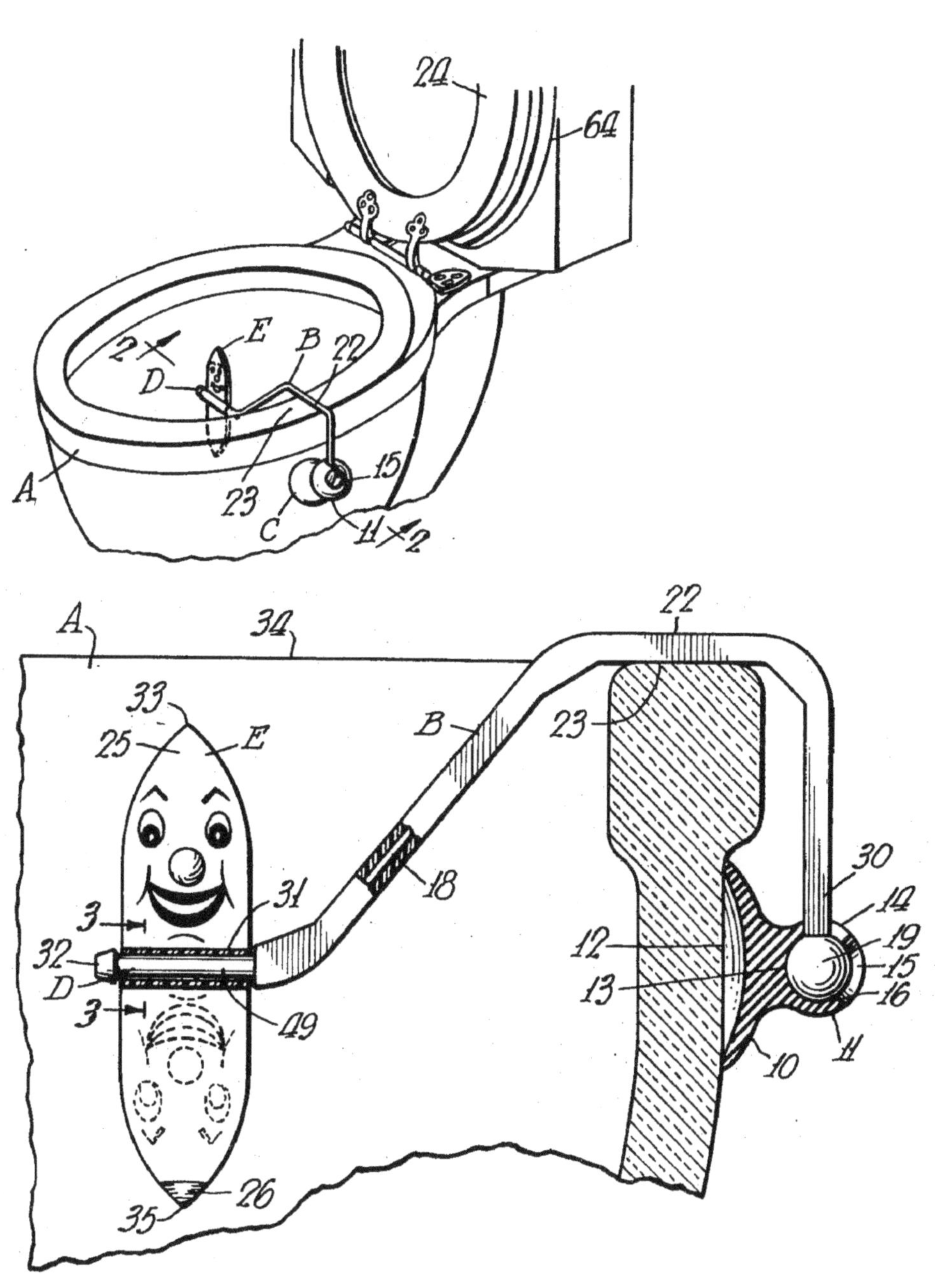

Dust Cover for Dogs

Kesh, Seroun, *Dust Cover for Dogs*, UNITED STATES PATENT OFFICE Patent No. 3,150,641, September 29, 1964.

It is well-known to animal lovers that dogs and cats harbor fleas and other pests and that the attempt to eradicate such pests oftentimes poses quite a problem. Efficient powders and sprays are now on the market for eliminating these pests, but their effective application and retention leaves much to be desired.

It is therefore an object of this invention to provide a device, which will greatly assist the animal owner, in the effective application and retention of such pesticides on the animal, for a period of time sufficient to do the work required.

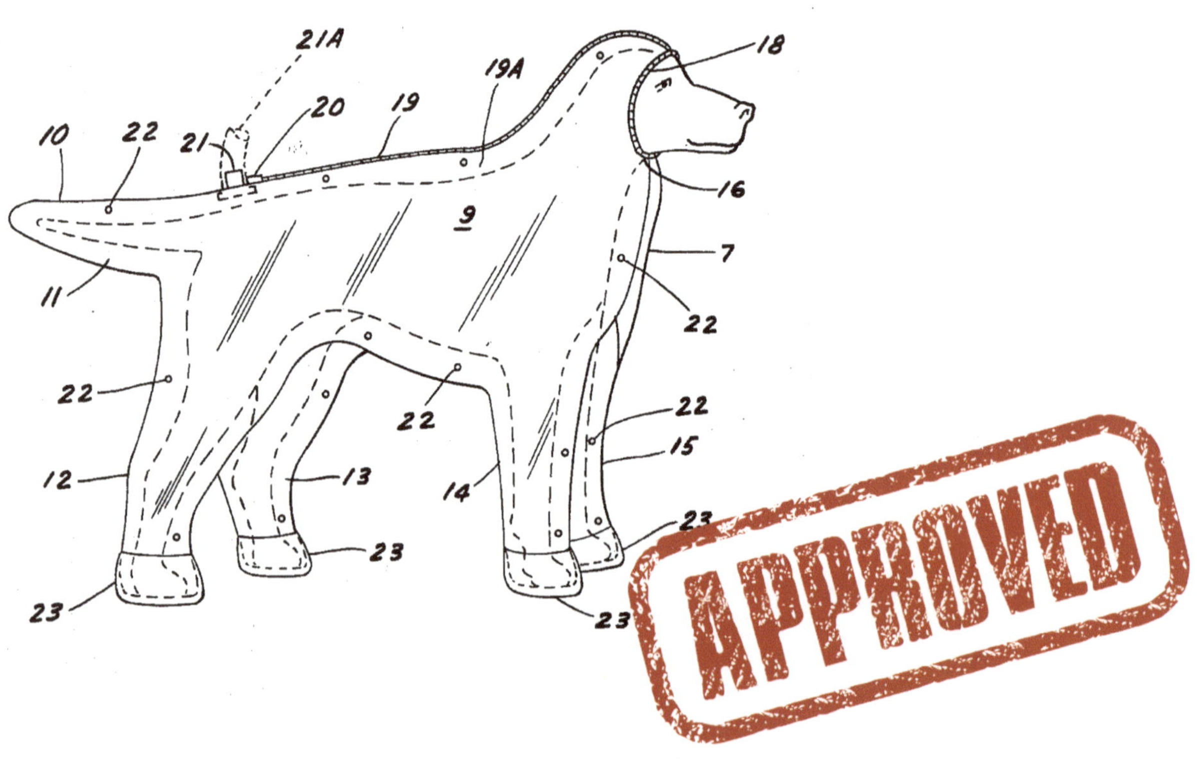

A NEW INSTRUMENT

for measuring the humidity of cavities

The new Clamometer of Prof. Uwe DIEGEL, created together with the eminent doctors SIFFREDI and DANIELS promises a new era of treatment for women's affections.

This device is useful for measuring the moisture of the clam and the intensity of contractions of the female orgasm.

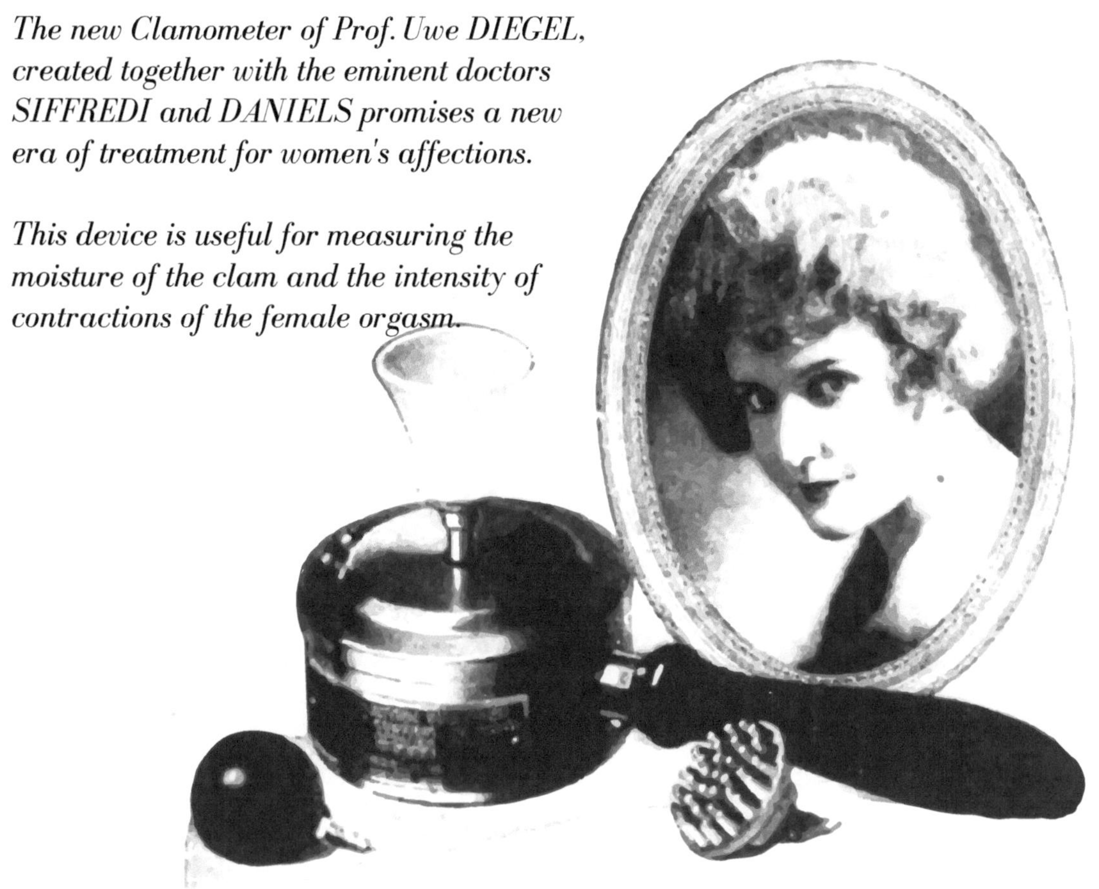

The CLAMOMETER is to the female cavity what the stethoscope is to the pulse

If I ask you point blank, my dear reader, what female sexuality is, you would probably be very embarrassed to answer me.

The symptoms by which the sexuality of women manifests itself -various disorders, pains, weakness, etc.- are not, in fact, a sufficient indication, for they are common to various illnesses. Headaches, poor blood circulation, almost all forms of physiological misery, resemble these prodromes, and the most erudite of doctors can be caught off-guard by these symptoms.

So, the first thing to do for the person suffering from the syndrome of frigidity is to put them on a diet, a severe diet, scrupulously studied, in order to provide for the expenses of the body, while regularly measuring the humidity of its cavities. It is advisable to prescribe to drink a lot - no strong alcohol, of course! (But champagnes of the MUMM and Veuve Clicquot brands are recommended) - to do leg exercises, massages, clitoral gymnastics, avoid excesses, emotions, overwork, - in resumé everything that it takes to overactivate combustion and remove impurities from the blood.

Whatever the real genesis of frigidity, on which the princes of science are far from having a unified opinion, the syndrome of female frigidity always results in a more or less profound disorder of the level of moisture in the vagina. It is therefore logical that if this humidity is measured and controlled, much of the problem will be resolved.

CONCLUSION: Prof. Uwe DIEGEL's **Clamometer** - which measures humidity *"like a ruler measures inches"* - is to be recommended to my eminent colleagues. It should be added that DIEGEL's Clamometer includes an **Orgasmatron** to measure the sexual satisfaction of the user and that it was the subject of two clinical publications: at the Academy of Sciences by Professor Rocco Siffredi, Doctor of Sexual Sciences, and at the Academy of Medicine by Dr. Stormy Daniels, Secondary Companion of the US President.

All doctors will understand me.
Dr. Michel CHAST

My esteemed colleagues recommend a regular measurement of the humidity of the sexual cavities (mouth, vagina, anus) to evaluate the risk of frigidity for insurance companies.

AVOID IMMITATIONS - FORMALLY DEMAND THE DIEGEL CLAMOMETER

Apparatus for Facilitating the Birth of a Child by Centrifugal Force

Blonsky, George B. et all, *Centrifugal Birther*, UNITED STATES PATENT OFFICE Patent No. 3,216,423, Nov 09, 1965.

The present invention relates to apparatus which utilizes centrifugal force to facilitate the birth of a child at less stress to the mother.

It is known, that due to natural anatomical conditions, the fetus needs the application of considerable propelling force to enable it to push aside the constricting vaginal walls, to overcome the friction of the uteral and vaginal surfaces and to counteract the atmospheric pressure opposing the emergence of the child. In the case of a woman who has a fully developed muscular system and has had ample physical exertion all through the pregnancy, as is common with all more primitive peoples, nature provides all the necessary equipment and power to have a normal and quick delivery. This is not the case, however, with more civilized women who often do not have the opportunity to develop the muscles needed in confinement.

It is the primary purpose of the present invention to provide an apparatus which will assist the under-equipped woman by creating a gentle, evenly distributed, properly directed, precision-controlled force, that acts in unison with and supplements her own efforts. In accordance with the invention, there is provided rotatable apparatus capable of subjecting the mother and the fetus to a centrifugal force directed to assist and supplement the efforts of the mother so that such centrifugal force and her efforts act in concert to overcome the action of resisting forces and facilitate the delivery of the child.

Apparatus for Facilitating the Birth of a Child by Centrifugal Force

Blonsky, George B. et all, *Centrifugal Birther*, UNITED STATES PATENT OFFICE Patent No. 3,216,423, Nov 09, 1965.

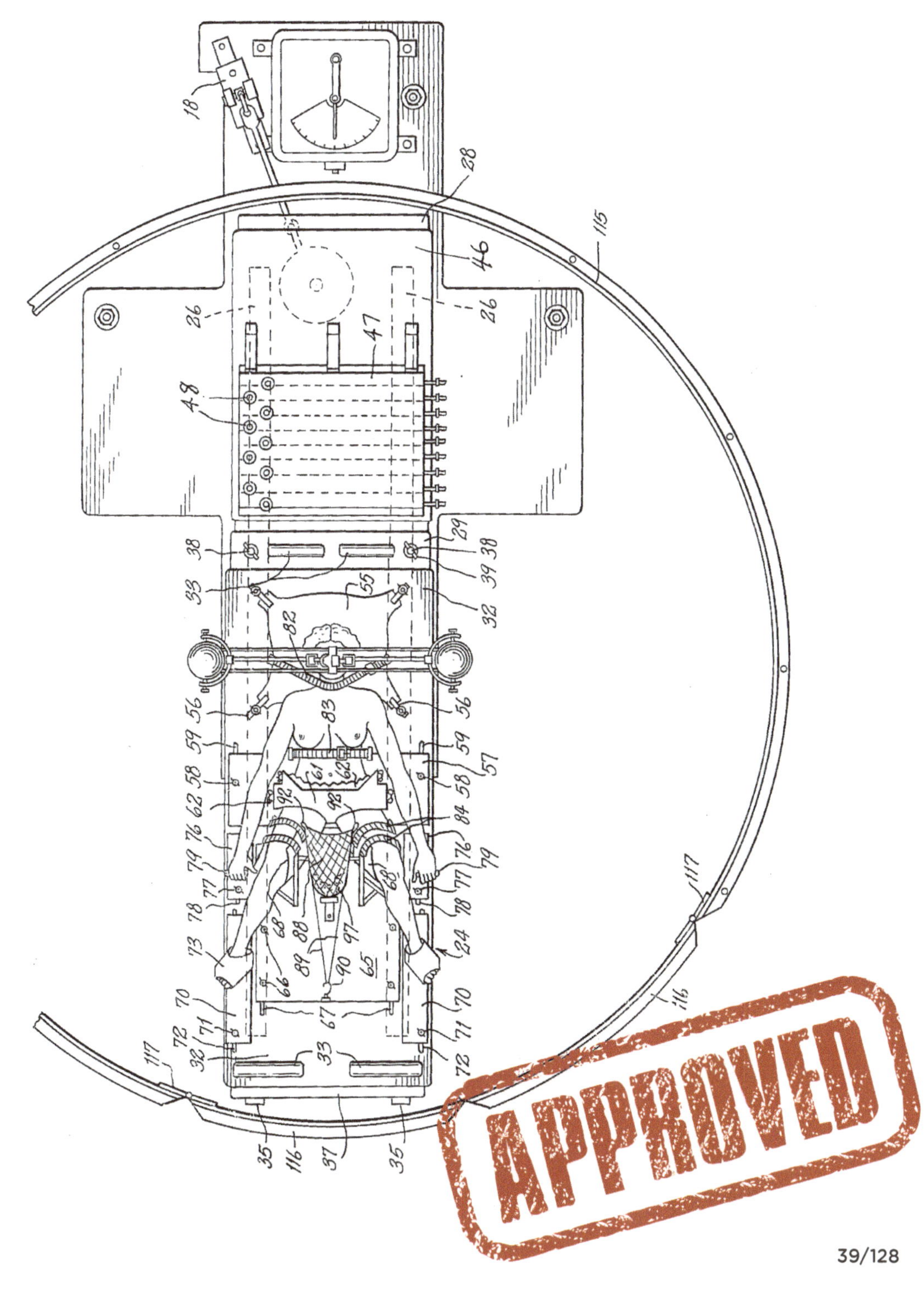

Cheese-Filter Cigarette

Stebbings, S. M., *Cheese-Filter Cigarette,* UNITED STATES PATENT Patent No. 3,234,948, Feb. 15, 1966.

This invention contemplates the provision of a cigarette filter which comprises particulate milk derived cheese used alone or in a mixture with particles of charcoal. By preference, the charcoal has been acid washed.

In order that the cheese may comprise small and well defined particles between which the smoke can pass freely, it is preferred to use a hard cheese as exemplified by Parmesan, Romano or Swiss cheese. Aged cheddars and other "hard' cheeses may also be used, particularly if partially dehydrated to facilitate grating, it being important that the cheese be particulate.

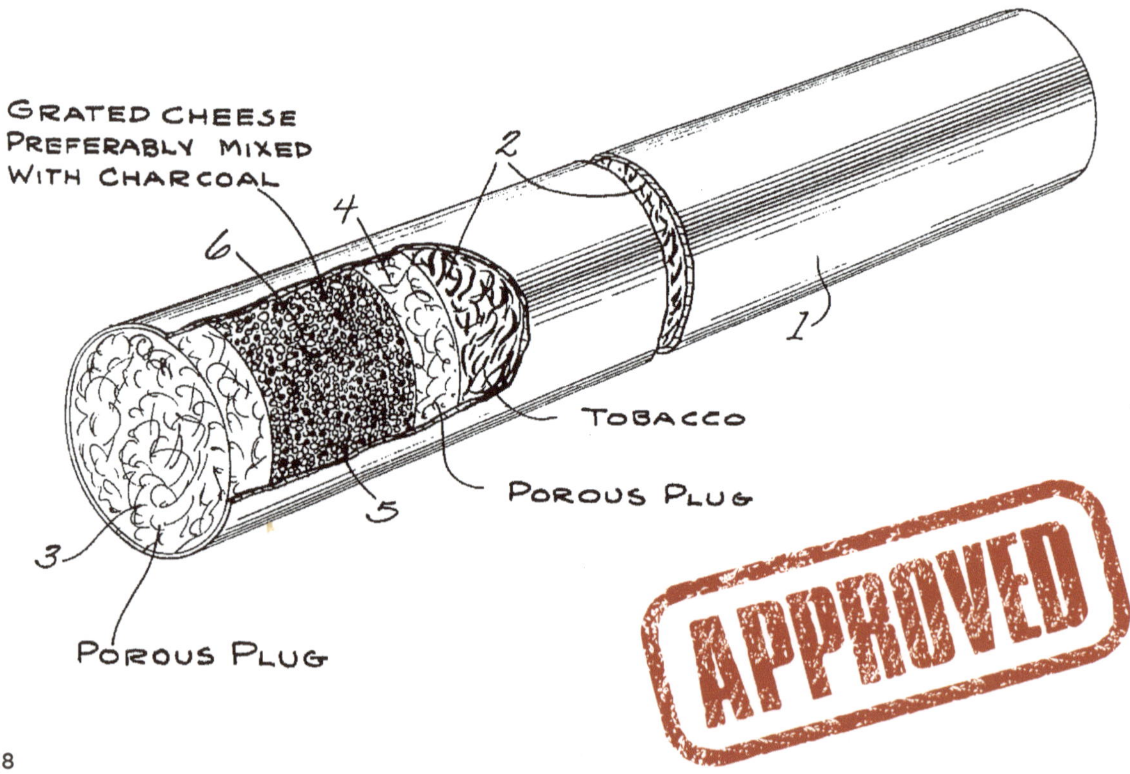

Animal Track Footwear Soles

McMorrow Philip E., *Animal Track Footwear Soles*, UNITED STATES PATENT OFFICE Patent No. 3,402,485, Sept. 24, 1968.

This invention relates to footwear for laying simulated animal tracks for either educational purposes or mere amusement. Because of the continuous depletion of the wildlife population of the world, it is becoming increasingly difficult to train wildlife experts, conservationists, forest rangers, Boy Scouts and the like in the art of tracking various wild animals.
Accordingly, it is an object of the present invention to provide means for simulating the tracks of various wild animals for the purpose of serious instruction or for games and amusement.

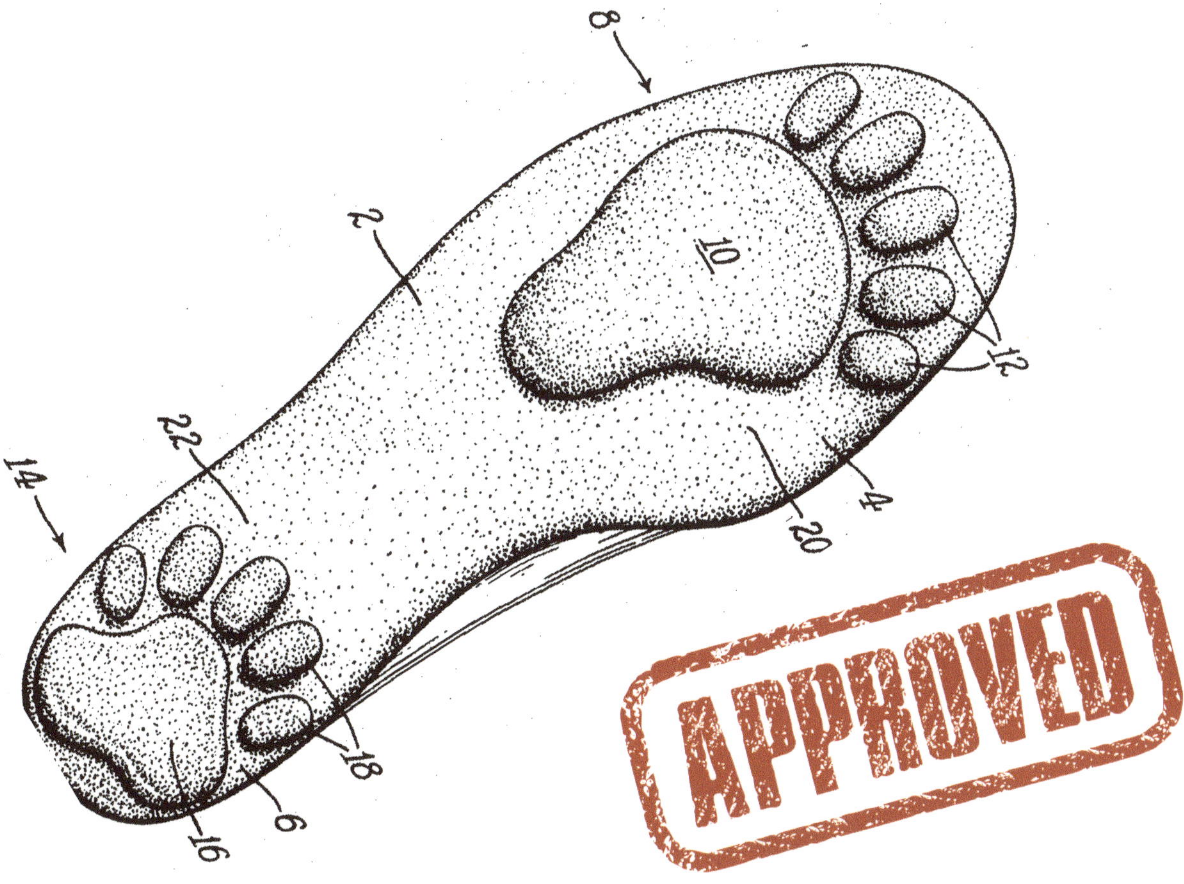

Automated Bathing Facility

Hallum, Gyda, *Automated Bathing Facility*, UNITED STATES PATENT OFFICE Patent No. 3,483,572, Dec. 16, 1969.

An automated bathing system or facility adapted for use in bathing large numbers of patients or persons in standing position by which the patients are suspended by means of a harness from an overhead rail and are moved along a conveyor belt floor past a wetting station, a soaping station, a rinsing station and finally into a drying station where the patient is air dried still in standing position and is readied for redressing under conditions that minimize the danger of infirm or mentally incapacitated injuring themselves or others by struggling during the bathing procedure and that provide improved sanitation in that all steps of the bathing procedure are accomplished with the patient in a standing position such that wash cloths and towels are not needed.

Automated Bathing Facility

Hallum, Gyda, *Automated Bathing Facility*, UNITED STATES PATENT OFFICE Patent No. 3,483,572, Dec. 16, 1969.

ILLUSTRATION

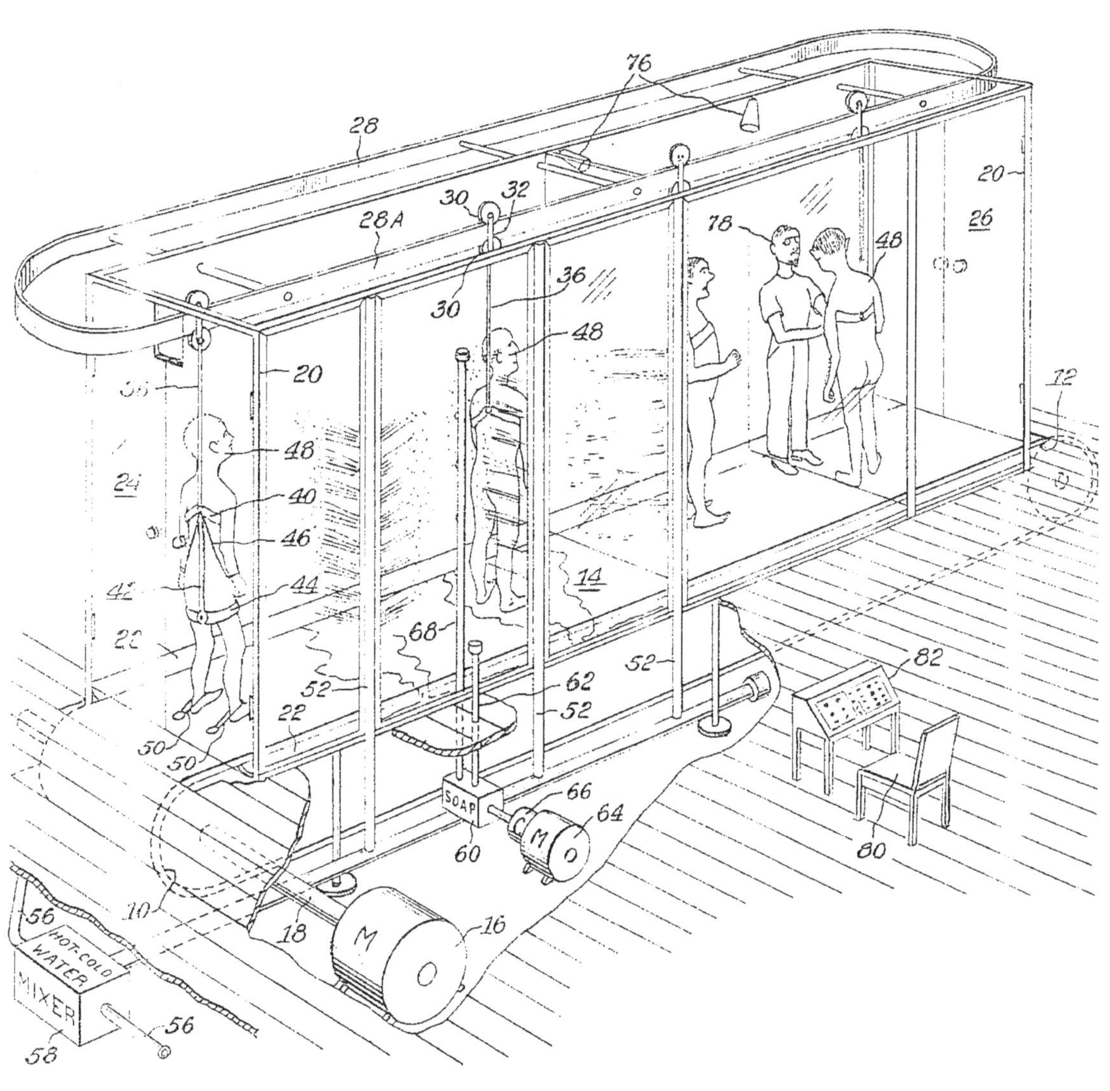

Water Vehicle

Vlad, J. John, *Water Vehicle*, UNITED STATES PATENT Patent No. 3,638,598, Feb. 01, 1972.

A water vehicle on which a rider may be towed by a boat or the like either on or beneath the surface of the water. The water vehicle comprises a substantially U-shaped frame member having the arm members of a pair of plane or planar members rotatably mounted to each leg thereof and including a pair of handles carried by each arm member to permit the rider of the water vehicle to independently rotate the planes relative to one another and to the frame member to thereby control the motion of the water vehicle while it is being towed by the boat. The ends of each leg of the U-shaped frame member are curved outwardly therefrom and are adapted to cooperate with the arm handles to permit the water vehicle to be mounted to the sides of a boat or the like whereby the water vehicle functions as a ladder to permit entry into the boat.

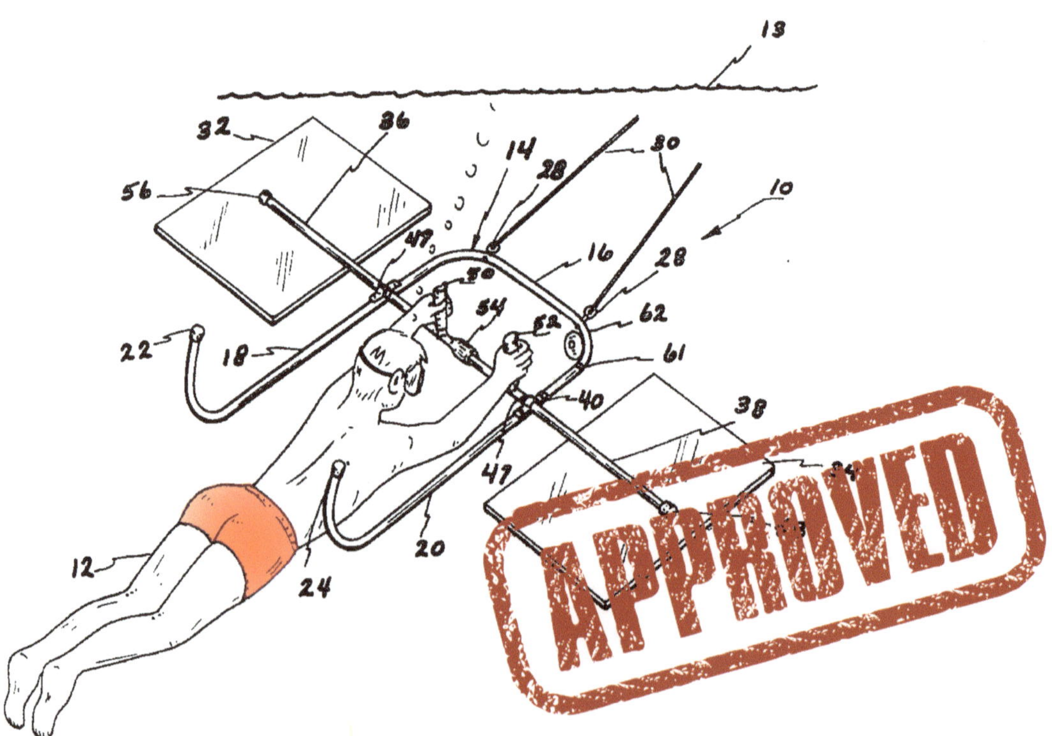

Wind car

Ferino, Ferdinand, *Wind car*, UNITED STATES PATENT Patent No. 3,724,577, Apr. 03, 1973.

A vehicle for traveling upon the ground, the vehicle including a pair of front wheels mounted in tandem side by side arrangement and a singular rear wheel, a pair of wings above the body and a fin rudder, the vehicle normally travelling at lower speed with all three wheels engaging the ground, the vehicle after attaining a 40 mile per hour speed then travelling upon only the rear wheel engaging the ground while the front wheels retract upwardly, balance being provided to the vehicle by means of the wings, together with the fin rudder.

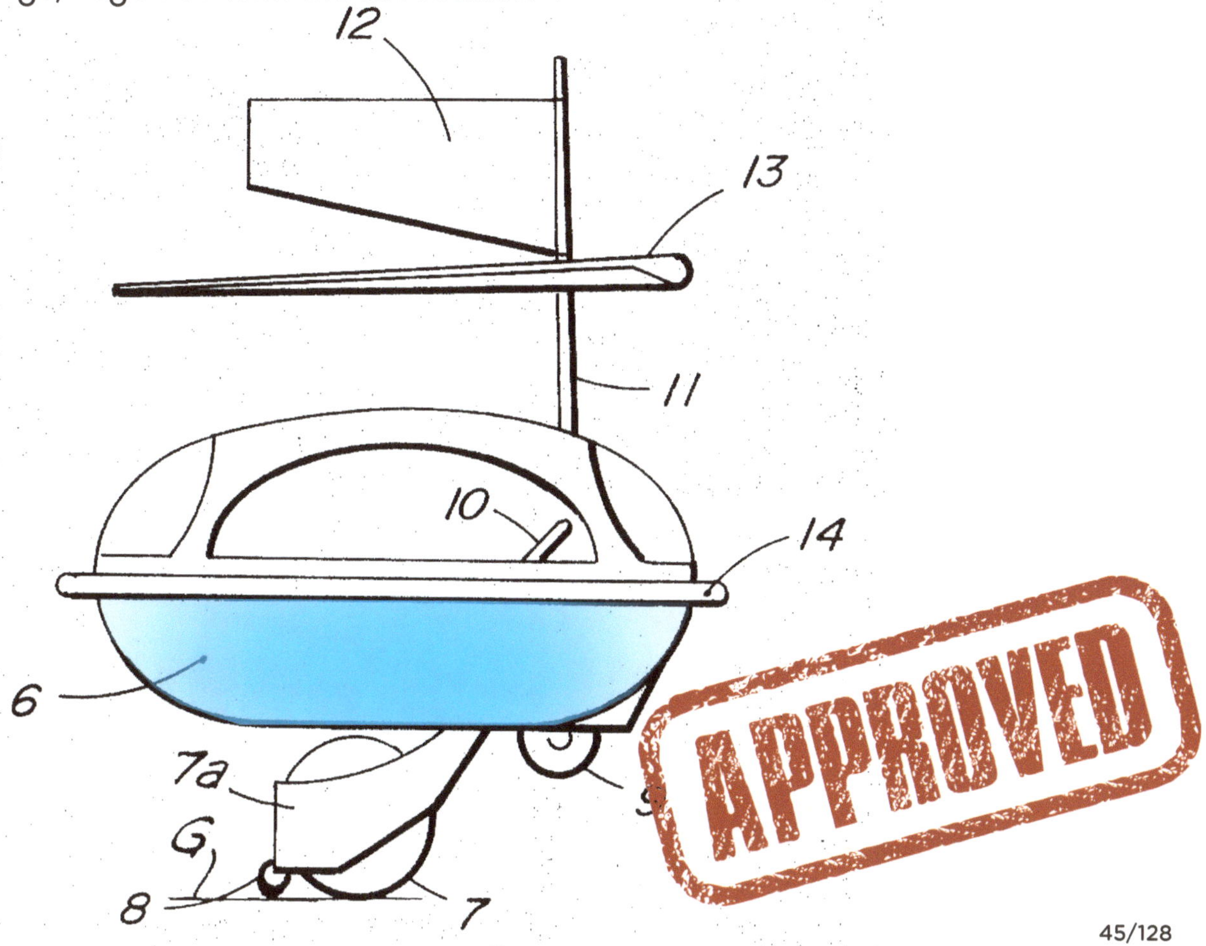

Breast-Shaped Pillow

De Rue, Monica P., *Breast Shaped Pillow*, UNITED STATES PATENT Patent No. Des. 237,569, November 11, 1975.

The ornamental design for a breast-shaped pillow, as shown and described.

DESCRIPTION
The ornamental design for a pillow, substantially as shown and described, it being understood that the broken lines are for illustrative purposes only and form no part of the claimed design.

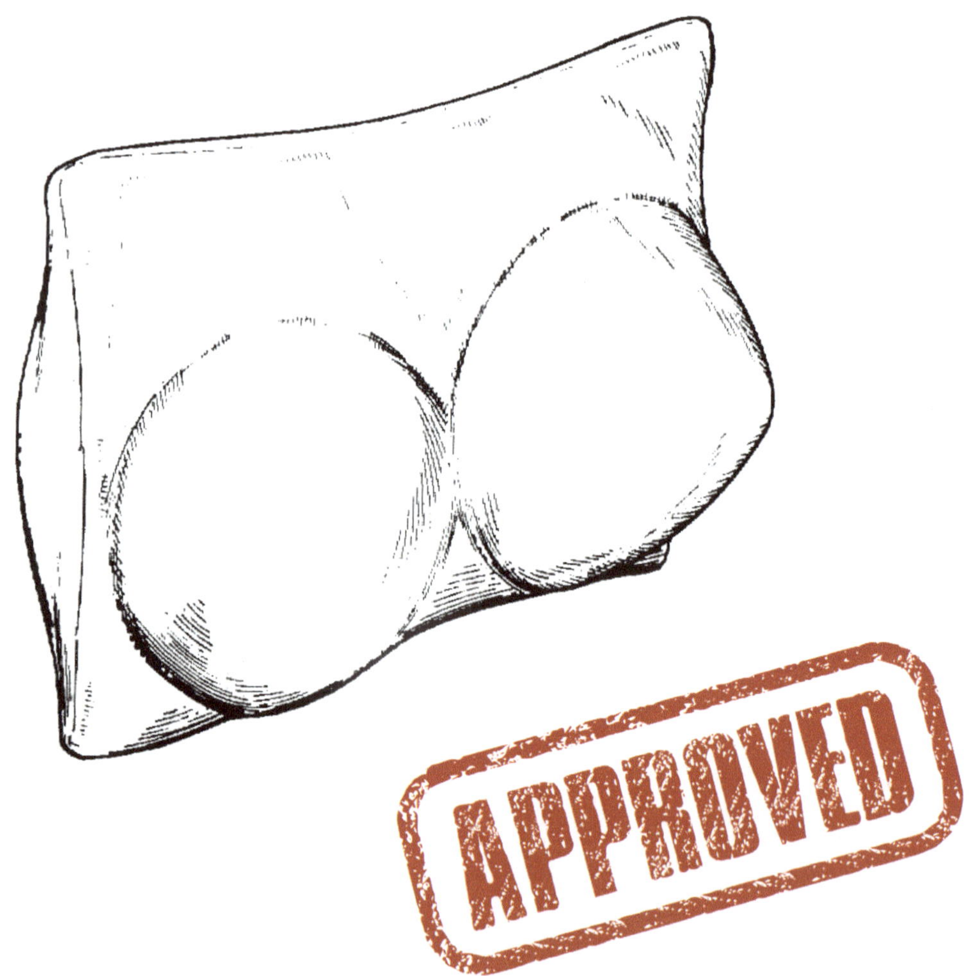

TV Control Device

Michaels, Chris T., *TV Control Device*, UNITED STATES PATENT Patent No. 3,962,748, June 15, 1976.

The present invention relates to a TV control device. More particularly, the invention relates to a TV control device for rotating a dial of a TV set from an area distant from the set.

A rod-like member of variable adjustable length has a handle at one end. A head part at the opposite end of the member cooperates with the dial of a TV set in a manner whereby a user in an area distant from the set selectively rotates the dial via the member.

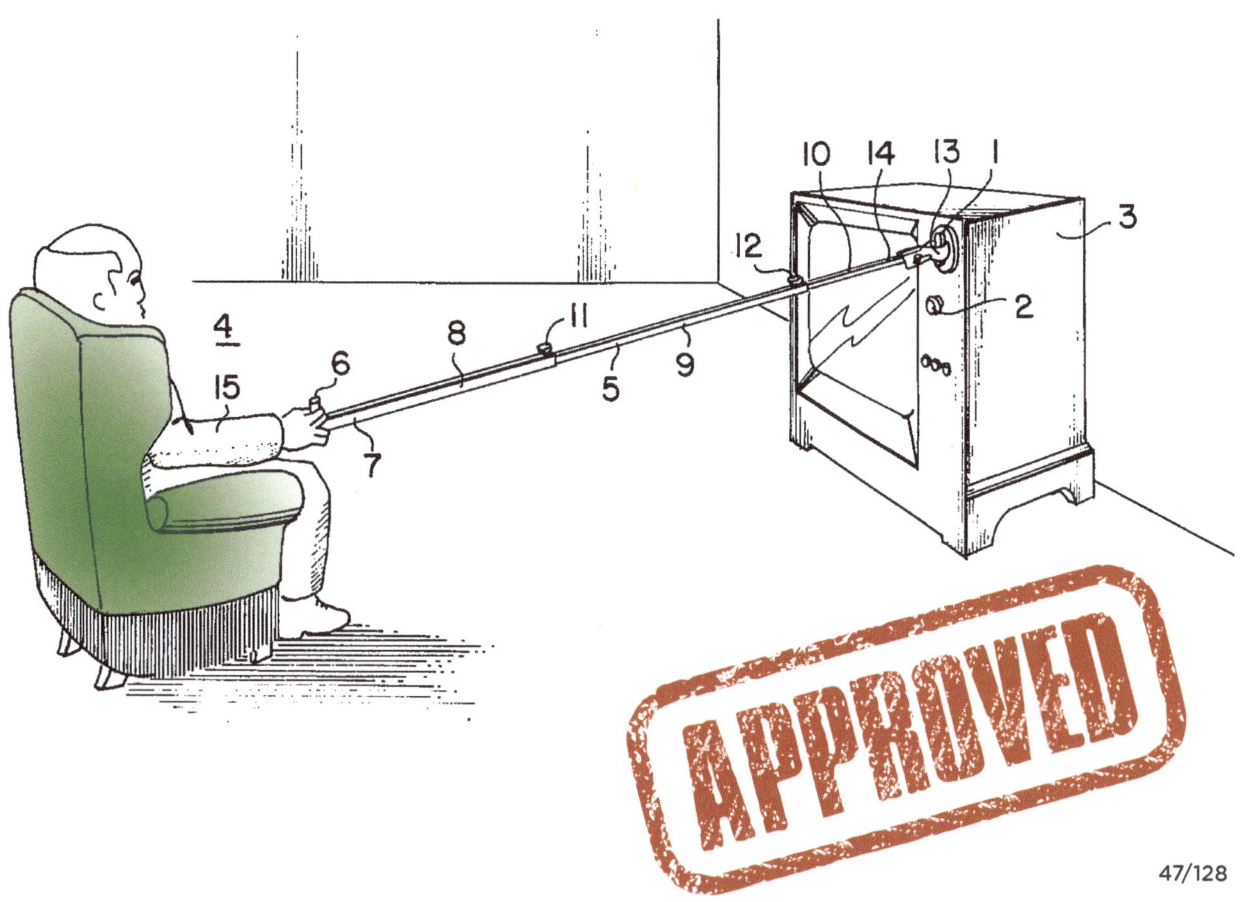

Spherical Rolling Hull Marine Vessel

Dandini, Alessandro, O., *Spherical Rolling Hull Marine Vessel*, UNITED STATES PATENT Patent No. 3,933,115, Jan. 20, 1976.

A marine vessel with a spherical rolling hull having a rotatably mounted shaft disposed through the horizontal poles of the sphere. A frame assembly is rigidly fixed to the shaft on the interior of the sphere for carrying a propulsion apparatus and cargo. The propulsion apparatus operates to turn wheels supporting the frame assembly and running upon a pair of annular tracks on the sphere's interior surface so as to cause the sphere to rotate. This rotational effect propels the vessel by means of fins or paddles on the outer surface of the sphere. Air propellers, elevators, and rudders to assist in navigation are mounted on the exterior of a pair of elongated cabins which are detachably connected to the shaft's terminals at the sides of the hull. Cargo and passengers are carried by these cabins which also can serve as independently powered, seaworthy marine vessels when detached from the mother ship. To expedite the handling of cargo, elevators are provided in the undercarriage of each cabin.

Pantyhose with Shaping Band for Cheeky Derriere Relief

Newmar, Julie, *Pantyhose with Shaping Band for Cheeky Derriere Relief*, UNITED STATES PATENT Patent No. 4,003,094, Jan 18, 1977.

The present invention provides pantyhose of a resilient stretchable fabric which enhance natural shape of a wearer's derriere giving it cheeky relief, rather than boardlike flatness. The pantyhose include a rear panty portion which covers and confines the wearer's buttocks. An elastic shaping band is attached to the rear panty portion and is connected from the vicinity of the wearer's crotch zone rearward to the vicinity of a waist band of the pantyhose. The elastic shaping band fits between the wearer's buttocks to produce the desired cheeky relief thereof.

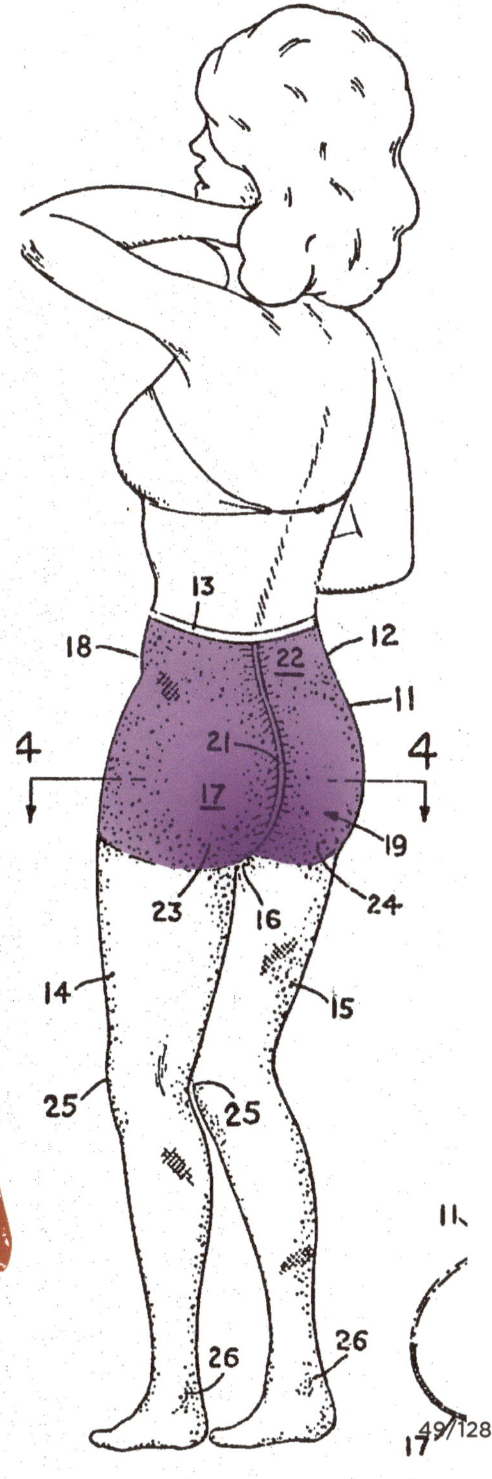

Target In Urinal To Attract Attention Of Urinating Males

Kreiss, Joel S., *Target In A Bowl Or Urinal To Attract The Attention Of Urinating Human Males*, UNITED STATES PATENT Patent No. 4,044,405, Aug. 30, 1977.

The present invention teaches a novel target structure which may be positioned low in the bowl of a toilet or a urinal and which will not have to be removed or rendered inoperative when the toilet is cleaned or used for purposes other than male urination. The present invention teaches a target which can be kept submerged in the toilet or bowl and will not be affected by either the flushing fluid or the urine or other substances commonly found to be flushed in toilets or urinals.

The present invention teaches a target which is safe, sanitary and which does not require independent cleaning.

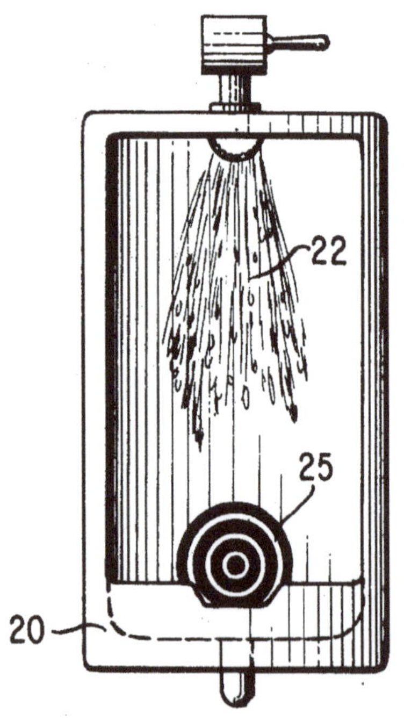

Object-Dispensing Wearing Apparel

Nemirofsky, Frank R., *Object-Dispensing Wearing Apparel*, UNITED STATES PATENT Patent No. 4,120,053, Oct. 17, 1978.

A portion of an article of clothing is provided with a sheet of material that is placed in confronting relation with and affixed to an inner surface of the portion to form a pocket for holding a number of novelty-type objects. An aperture is formed in an outer surface of the portion to communicate the outer surface to the pocket and to allow the objects contained therein to be dispensed therefrom. The outer surface is provided with an illustrative design that draws a viewer's attention to and suggests the aperture as a dispensing point for the objects.

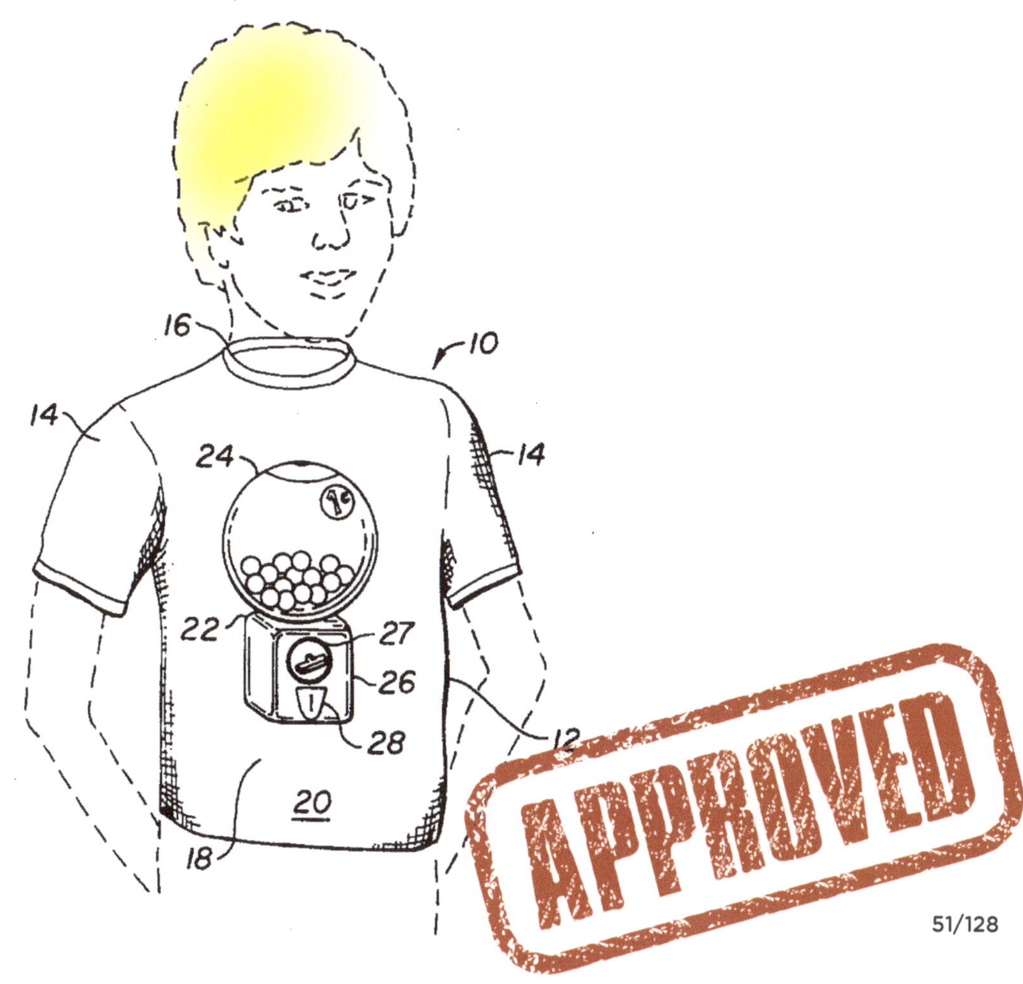

Automobile Protector

Spencer, William, *Automobile Protector*, UNITED STATES PATENT Patent No. 4,154,254, May 15, 1979.

A cover which may be removably installed over a vehicle including a shroud mounted on an umbrella-like frame which fits in close relationship to a vehicle to be covered. The frame may include a plurality of supports or ribs extending outwardly from a central hub and downwardly so as to generally encompass a vehicle which may be covered.

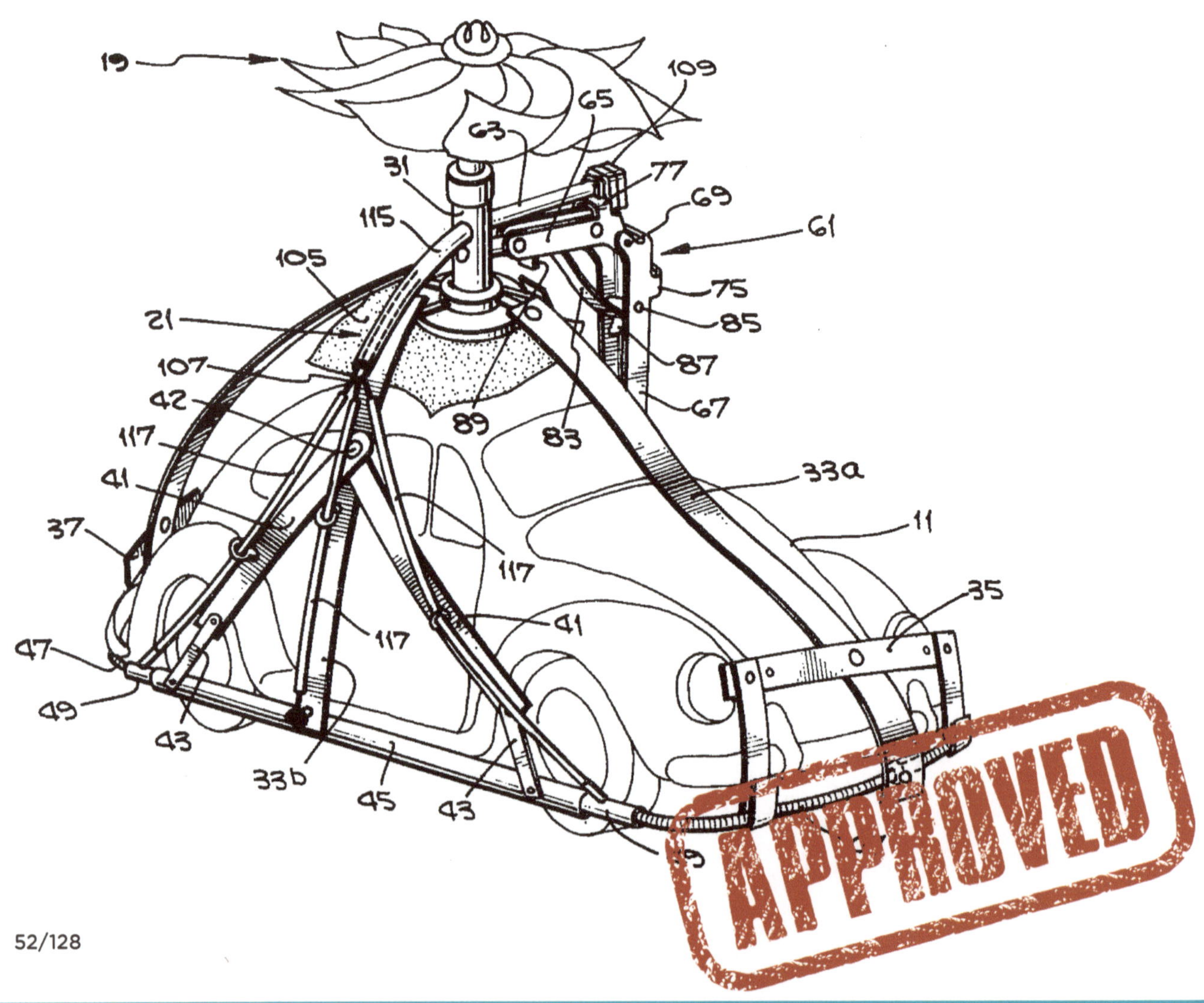

Bird Trap and Cat Feeder

Voelker, Leo O., *Bird Trap and Cat Feeder,* UNITED STATES PATENT Patent No. 4,150,505, Apr. 24, 1979.

The invention solves the problem of reducing the population of sparrows. Heretofore, the ordinary sparrow has greatly proliferated, thereby taking the place of more popular birds, such as the canary, blue bird, wren, swallow, and other birds that are appealing to the eye and enjoyable to listen to. Also, because of the increased population of the sparrow, the bird has become a nuisance due to bird droppings, the building of nests, and the taking of food supplies which would ordinarily be enjoyed by other birds.

The invention provides means for continuously trapping sparrows and supplying a cat and neighborhood cats with a supply of sparrows. The cat feeder by its design is self-cleaning since the cat quickly learns to remove the sparrow from the cage.

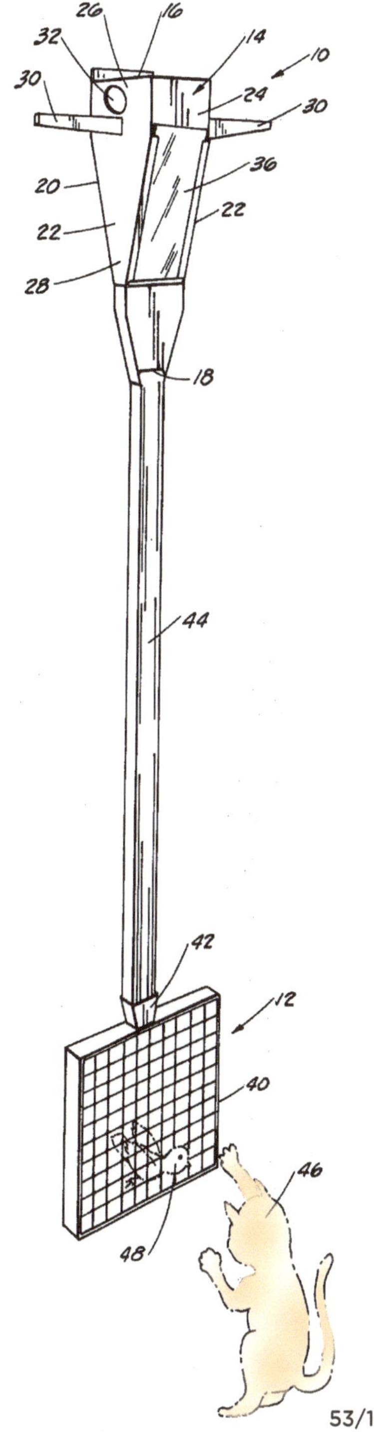

Body Mounted Umbrella

Morman, John W., *Body Mounted Umbrella*, UNITED STATES PATENT Patent No. 4,188,965, Feb. 19, 1980.

A collapsible umbrella shade is mounted to the body of the user by means of a belt to which a vertical post is pivoted. A shaft carrying the shade is pivoted to the top end of the post and may be folded downwardly to a compact storage position. During use, a removable pin maintains the shaft in an extended position wherein it forms an upward continuation of the post to locate the umbrella shade directly overhead. A pair of springs stabilize the post in its normal upright position, while wire arms serve as handles for displacing the post in order to provide already access to the pin and the operating mechanism for opening and closing the umbrella shade.

Thumb Twiddler

Knowles, Horace A., *Thumb Twiddler*, UNITED STATES PATENT Patent No. 4,227,342, Aug. 17, 1980.

There has been known from time immemorial the idle pastime of what is commonly called "twiddling the thumbs." This relaxing pastime consists of the rotation of two thumbs about another, i.e., orbitally about an imaginary axis between the two thumbs. The forefingers of one hand are usually clasped by the forefingers of the other hand during thumb-twiddling.

Heretofore no equipment has been available to the thumb twiddler to assist him in the twiddling procedure. The Thumb Twiddler is a novelty toy used to facilitate thumb twiddling that comprises a pair of closely spaced, parallel, tubular holes each adapted to receive the first digit of a thumb, the walls of the holes being smooth and slippery, and of diameter slightly larger than the thumbs. The thumbs are inserted into the holes and are rotated orbitally about an imaginary axis between the two holes.

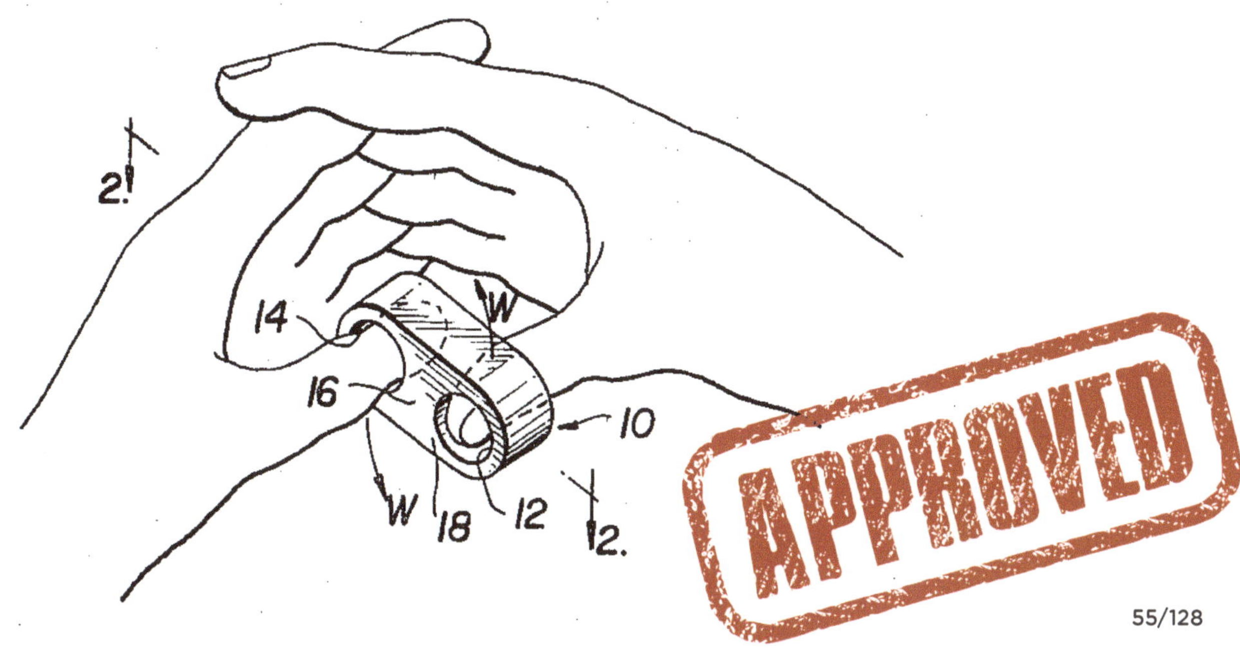

Animal Ear Protectors

Williams, James D., *Animal Ear Protectors* UNITED STATES PATENT Patent No. 4,233,942, Nov. 18,1980.

This invention provides a device for protecting the ears of animals, especially long-haired dogs, from becoming soiled by the animal's food while the animal is eating. The device provides a generally tubular shaped member for containing and protecting each ear of the animal, and a member to position the tubular member and ani mal ears away from the mouth and food of the animal while it is eating.

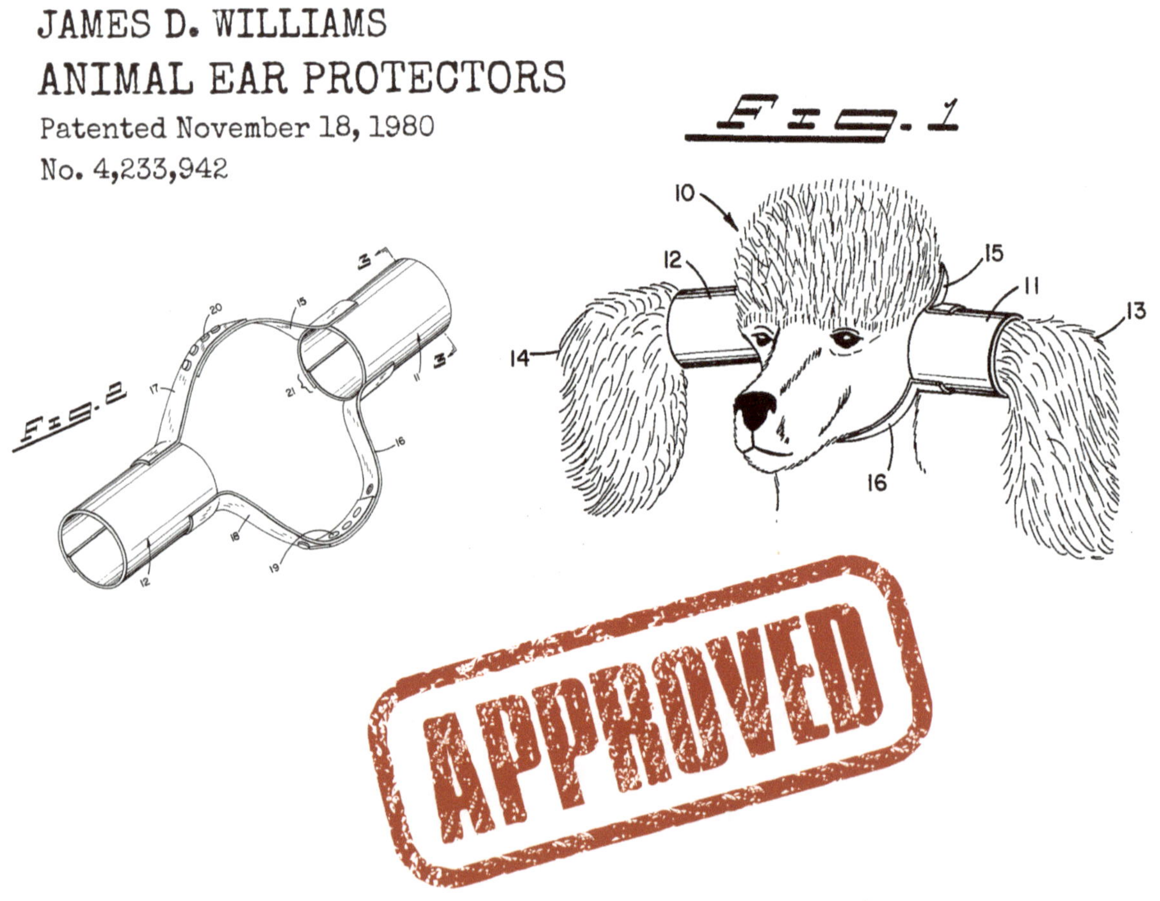

Exercising Device for Water Use

Mansolill, Ralph A. and Kathryn R., *Exercising Device for Water Use*, UNITED STATES PATENT Patent No. 4,241,688, Dec. 30, 1980.

A device useful for exercising in a swimming pool or other body of water which allows the person to be supported in a substantially seated upright position in the body of water such that the neck, head and upper shoulders of the person remain out of the water, allowing the person to exercise the legs, arms and torso while neutrally buoyant.

Animal Powered Drive Means

Barnes, Phillip Arthur., *Animal Powered Drive Means.* UK Patent Application (19) GB (11) 2 060 081 A, 29 Apr 1981.

A road vehicle is driven by animal powered drive means comprising an endless conveyor belt acting as a tread-mill and driving the vehicle drive wheels through a chain, a clutch, and a variable-ratio gearbox. The belt is centered on the longitudinal centre line of the vehicle below an enclosure for the animal, driver and passenger spaces being on either side of the enclosure. The animal is supported by harness including a collar, trace, a back strap, girth and a breeching box. Containers are provided to collect droppings.

There are several advantages in taking the horse off the road surface in vehicle propulsion. The most obvious is speed variation. The drive connection between the endless belt and the road wheels can include a gearbox with a number of different ratios available. By selecting the lowest gear the vehicle moves forward slower than the walking speed of the horse; this helps it to pull a load up hill. By selecting the highest gear the vehicle moves faster than the walking speed of the horse and so shortens the journey time.

Animal Powered Drive Means

Barnes, Phillip Arthur., *Animal Powered Drive Means.* UK Patent Application (19) GB (11) 2 060 081 A, 29 Apr 1981.

ILLUSTRATION

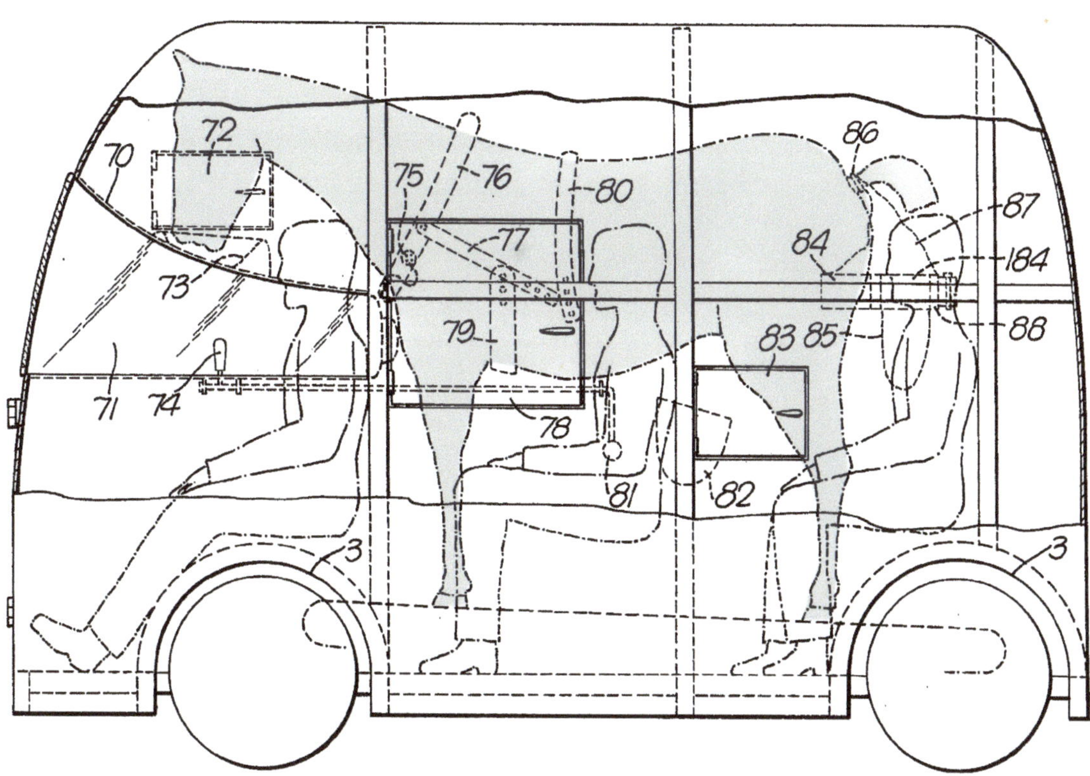

The horse has no control of the direction and speed of the vehicle, so that even if it is nervous in traffic it cannot bolt or shy. The space in which it stands ensures it cannot move its position to any material extent, so that it is possible to fix containers in the right position to prevent its droppings reaching the road.

Device for Moistening Stamps

Poynter, Donald B., *Device for Moistening the Adhesive Coatin on Postage Stamps and Envelopes*, UNITED STATES PATENT Patent No. 4,300,473, Nov. 17, 1981.

Apparatus for moistening adhesive coatings on postage material and the like which includes an enclosure having a container of liquid therein. A plunger is provided to lift an absorbant applicator from the liquid and pass the applicator through an opening in the side of the enclosure. A closure member for the opening is opened in response to the applicator movement. The applicator may be in the form of a human tongue and the closure may be in the form of a human lip.

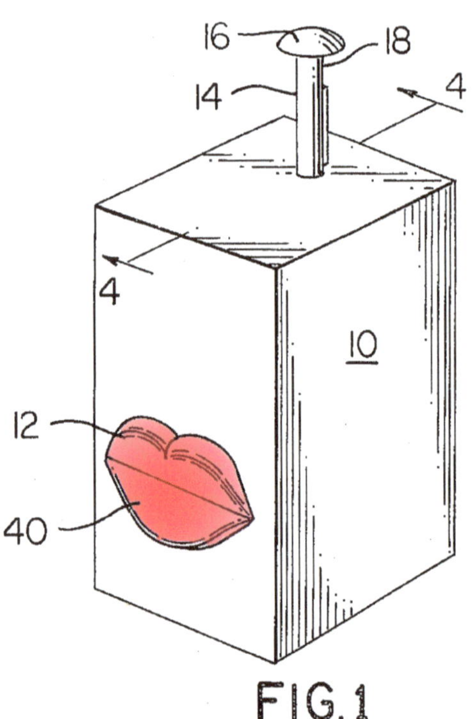

FIG.1

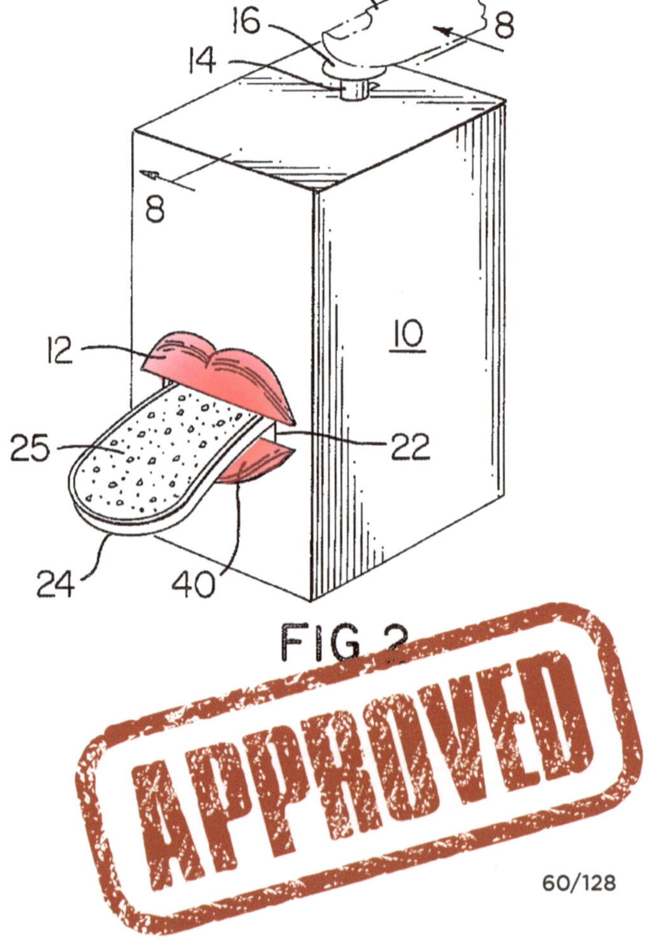

FIG 2

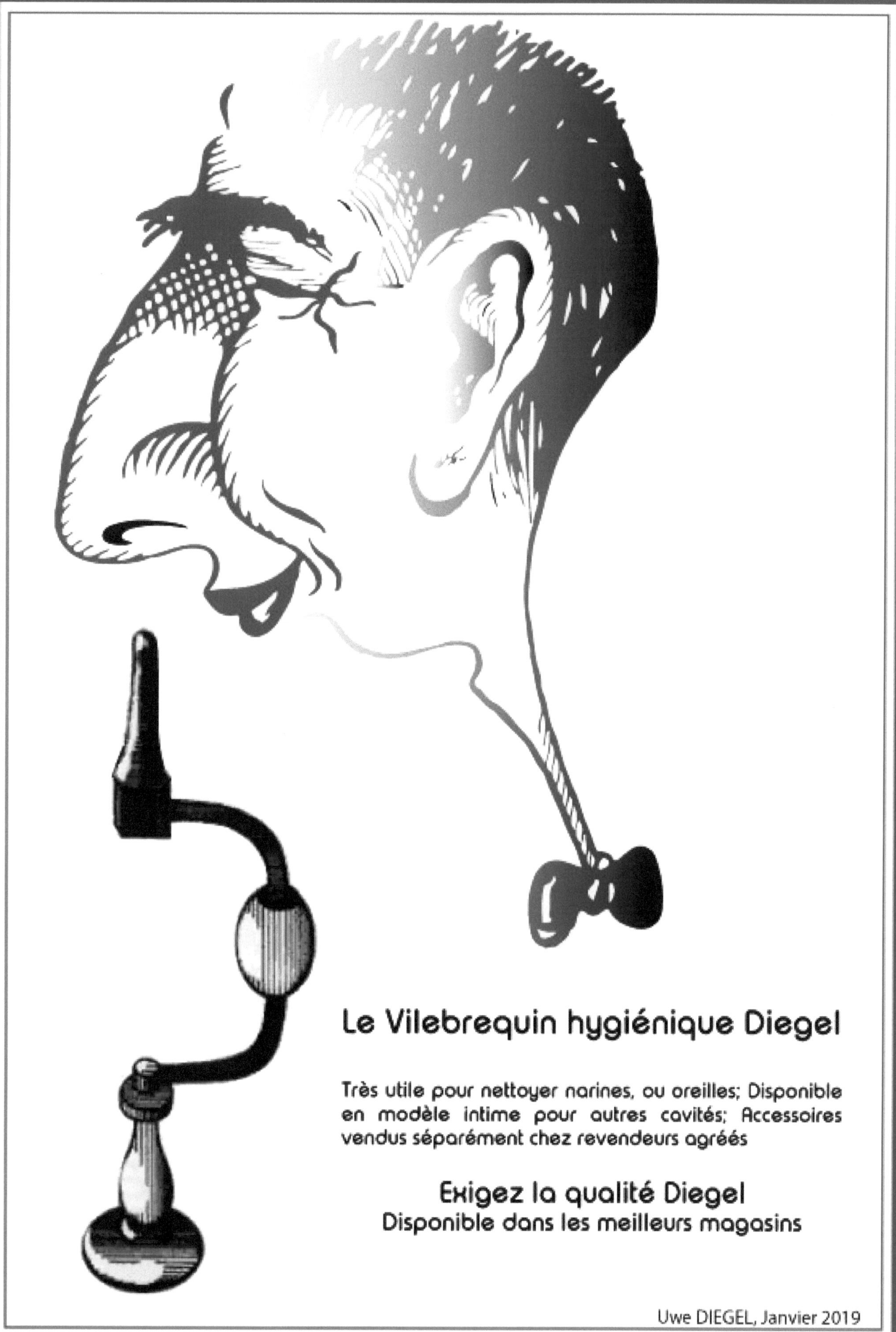

Le Vilebrequin hygiénique Diegel

Très utile pour nettoyer narines, ou oreilles; Disponible
en modèle intime pour autres cavités; Accessoires
vendus séparément chez revendeurs agréés

Exigez la qualité Diegel
Disponible dans les meilleurs magasins

Uwe DIEGEL, Janvier 2019

Anti Eating Face Mask

Barmby, Lucy L., *Anti Easting Face Mask,* UNITED STATES PATENT Patent No. 4,344,424, Aug. 17, 1982.

Obesity is a basic problem with which many people today are confronted and, as clearly indicated by the variety of diets proposed to conquer overweight the major contributing actor to overweight is the excessive consumption of food. The temptation to eat which leads one to eat excessively is ever present and the ready availability of attractively prepared, taste-tempting foods makes the temptation to eat and therefore over eat virtually irresistible. Frequently, this temptation is so great that compulsive eating is not uncommon and many persons are virtually without the strength of will to resist overeating. The average person, therefore, does have a problem as to the over consumption of food but, even worse, when certain individuals are exposed to food constantly such as chefs, cooks, restaurant personnel or the like, it is a foregone conclusion that these individuals will consume far more food than is proper particularly when such food is readily available at no cost.

This patent is for an anti-eating face mask which includes a cup-shaped member conforming to the shape of the mouth and chin area of the user, together with a hoop member and straps detachably engageable with a user's head for mounting the cup-shaped member in overlying relationship with the user's mouth and chin area under the nose thereby preventing the ingestion of food by the user.

Anti Eating Face Mask

Barmby, Lucy L., *Anti Easting Face Mask,* UNITED STATES PATENT Patent No. 4,344,424, Aug. 17, 1982.

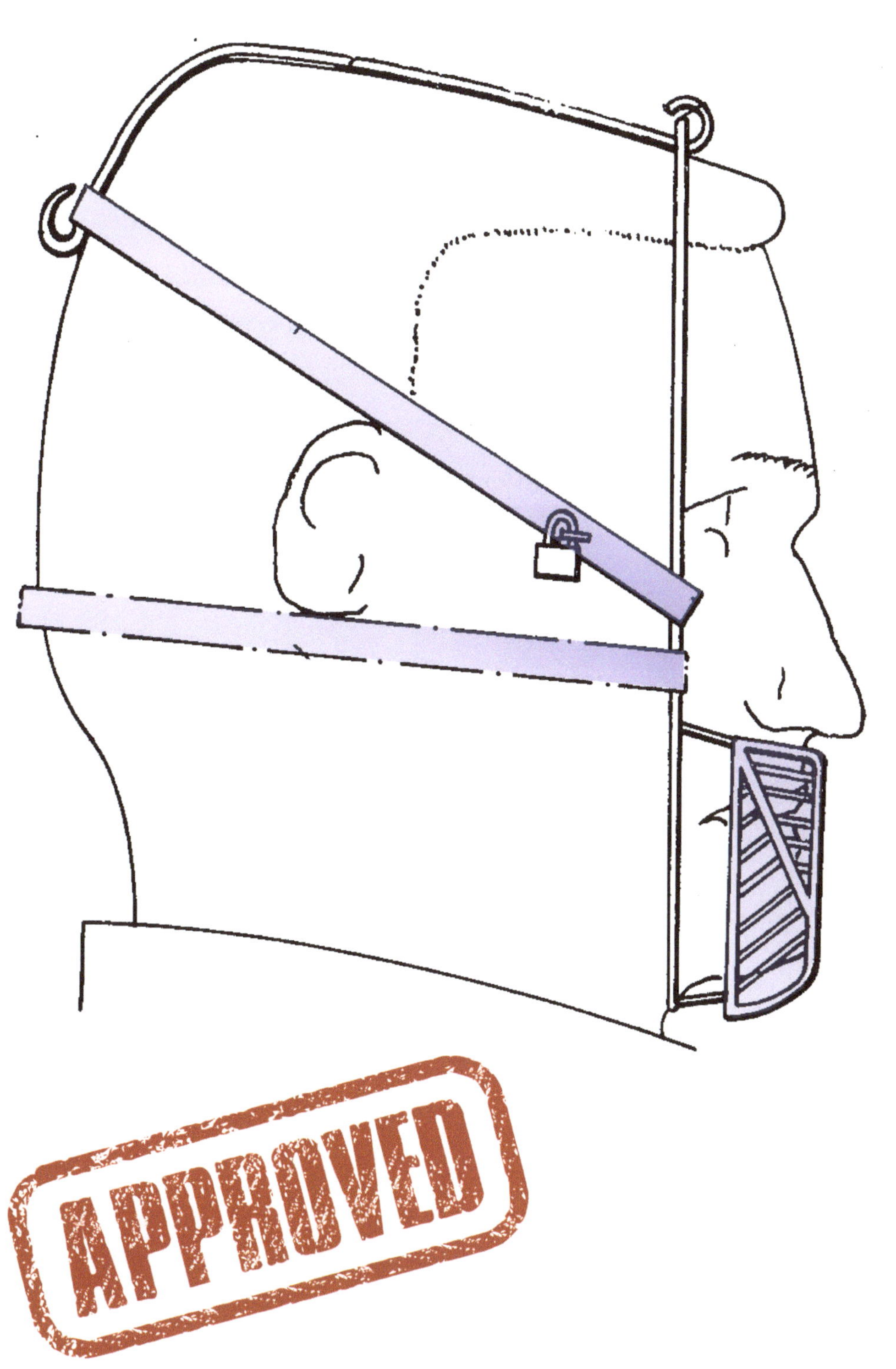

Pedal Operated Mower

Porath, Deanna F., *Pedal Operated Mower*, UNITED STATES PATENT Patent No. 4,455,816, Jun. 26, 1984.

A tricycle frame providing basic support for the pedal operated mower, pedals turning a forward sprocket for providing locomotion, the locomotion communicating by a chain to tum a rear sprocket mounted on a shaft having a set of split cutting blades peripheraUy disposed about the cutting shaft for turning the shaft and cutting blades, and gear means connecting the cutter shaft with rear wheels of the tricycle frame and resulting in the locomotion thereof. A protective shield is mounted on the tricycle frame to protect the operator from debris thrown up during the course of mowing, and also a set of goose neck handle bars, an appropriate sized front wheel and a large triangular padded seat are also provided in the combination.

Water Skis and Oaring Sticks

Gilber, Serge, *Water Skis and Oaring Sticks*, UNITED STATES PATENT Patent No. 4,527,984, Jun. 9, 1985.

The invention consists of a pair of water oaring sticks to be used in conjunction with flotation skis to be secured to the feet of a user, in order to facilitate the movement of the latter over aqueous surfaces. Each stick comprises a fixed or telescopically-extendable pole, having a handle mounted at one end and a float member at the other end to which an inclined paddle is secured.

Greenhouse Helmet

Anguita, Waldemar, *Greenhouse Helmet,* UNITED STATES PATENT. Patent No. 4,605,000, Aug. 12, 1986.

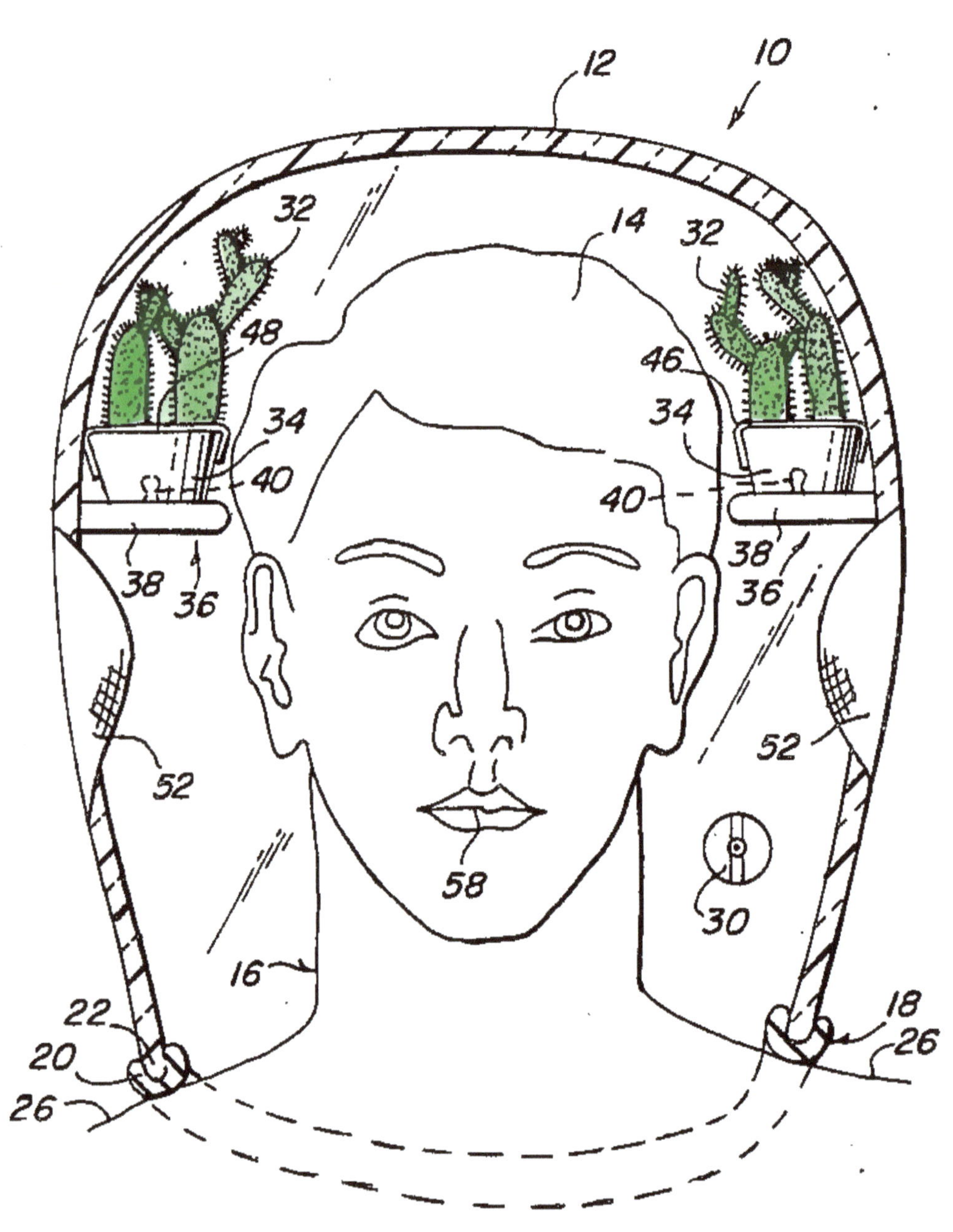

Greenhouse Helmet

Anguita, Waldemar, *Greenhouse Helmet,* UNITED STATES PATENT Patent No. 4,605,000, Aug. 12, 1986.

A greenhouse helmet is provided and consists of a dome containing plants secured within the dome worn completely over the head of a person so that the person can breathe in the oxygen given off by the plants.

Another object is to provide a greenhouse helmet that has air filters so that ambient air containing carbon dioxide will be filtered therethrough and mixed with the carbon dioxide breathed out by the person to be used by the plants.

An additional object is to provide a greenhouse helmet that will contain hearing and speaking devices so that the person can hear within and speak out through the helmet.

A further object is to provide a greenhouse helmet that is economical in cost to manufacture and that is simple and easy to use.

Back-Patting Apparatus

Piro, Ralph R., *Pat on the Back Apparatus*, UNITED STATES PATENT Patent No. 4,608,967, Sep. 2, 1986.

A self-congratulatory apparatus having a simulated human hand carried on a pivoting arm suspended form shoulder supported member. The hand is manually swingable into and out of contact with the user's back to give an amusing or an important pat-on-the-back.

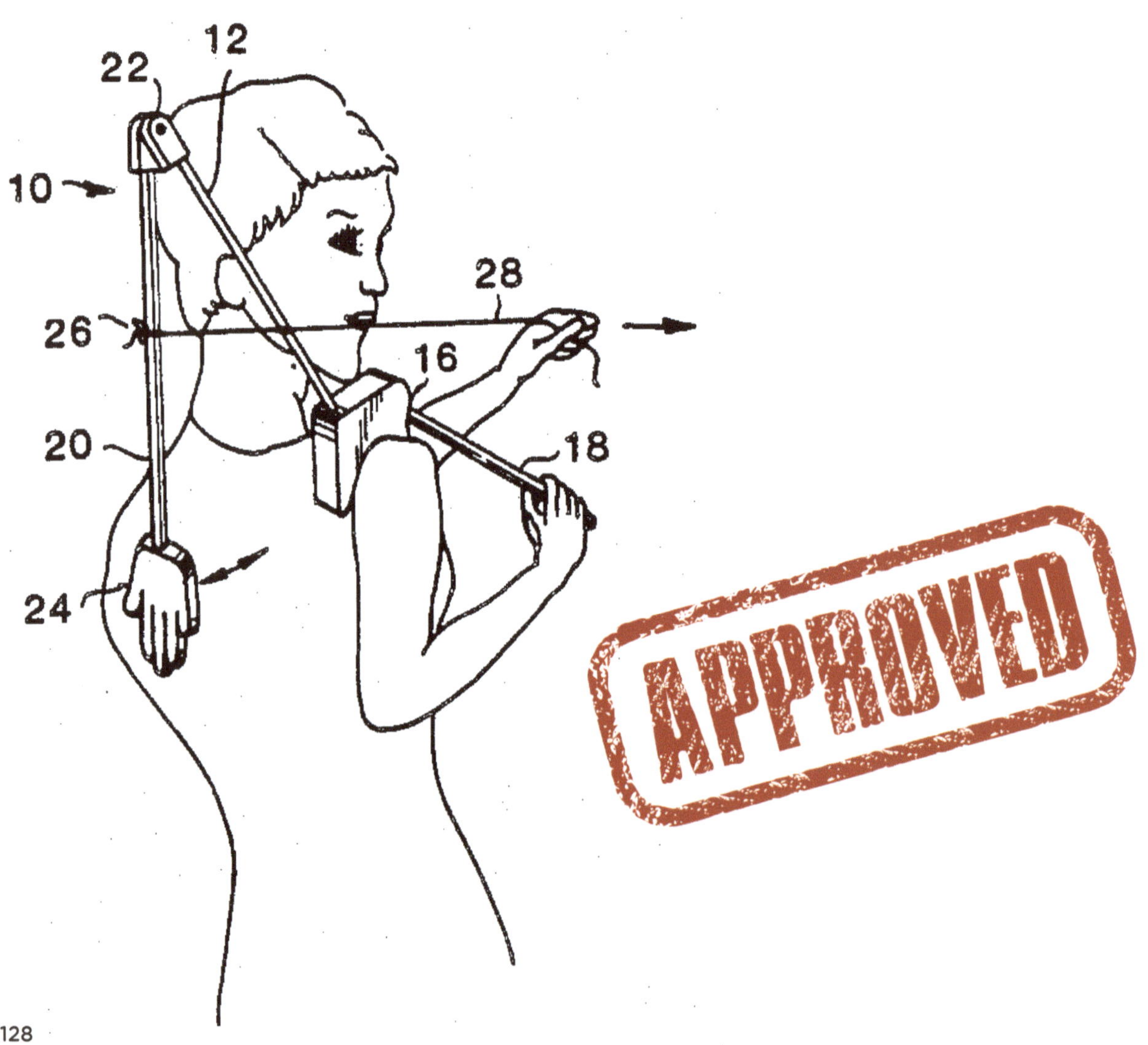

Monkey Emasculator

Davis, John W. , *Release Mechanism,* UNITED STATES PATENT Patent No. 4,634,021, Jan. 6, 1987.

A release mechanism is disclosed for releasing an object such as a ball from a body under the force of gravity. A bimetallic element obstructs or opens an opening in the body for retaining or releasing the object depending upon the temperature of the bimetallic element. The release mechanism may be incorporated into a novelty "brass monkey" for "emasculating" the monkey when the temperature decreases to a predetermined temperature at which the balls in the "brass monkey" are permitted to drop to a base which is designed to produce an audible sound when struck by the balls.

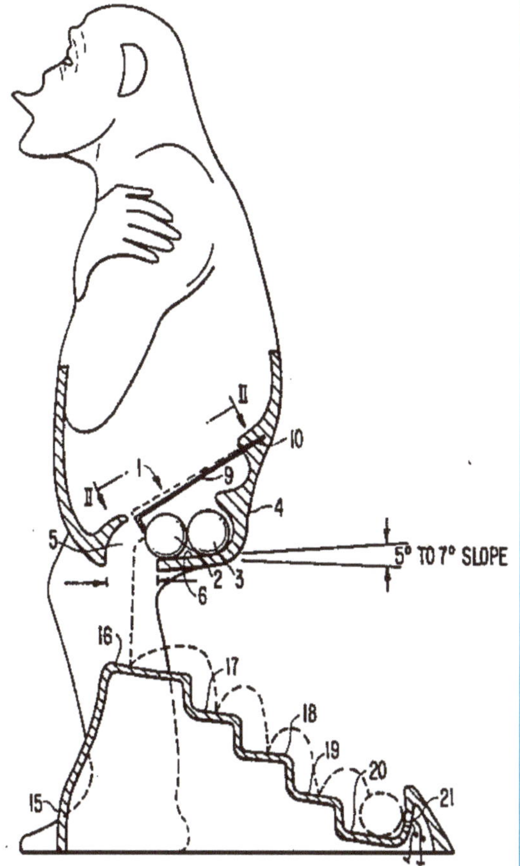

Facial Muscle Exercise Mask

Crawford, Johnathan G., *Facial Muscle Exercise Mask*, UNITED STATES PATENT Patent No. 4,666,148, May 19, 1987.

A facial exercise mask includes an externally convex mask body made of strong, lightweight plastic or acrylic. A central face portion has holes for eyes, nose, and mouth of the wearer. An inflatable lining for the inner surface of the mask at brow, temple, cheek, chin, and central portions, and having corresponding holes for the eyes, nose, and mouth is provided. Air is pumped between the lining and the inner surface of the mask body to inflate the lining which provides the resistive force for the facial muscles to work against.

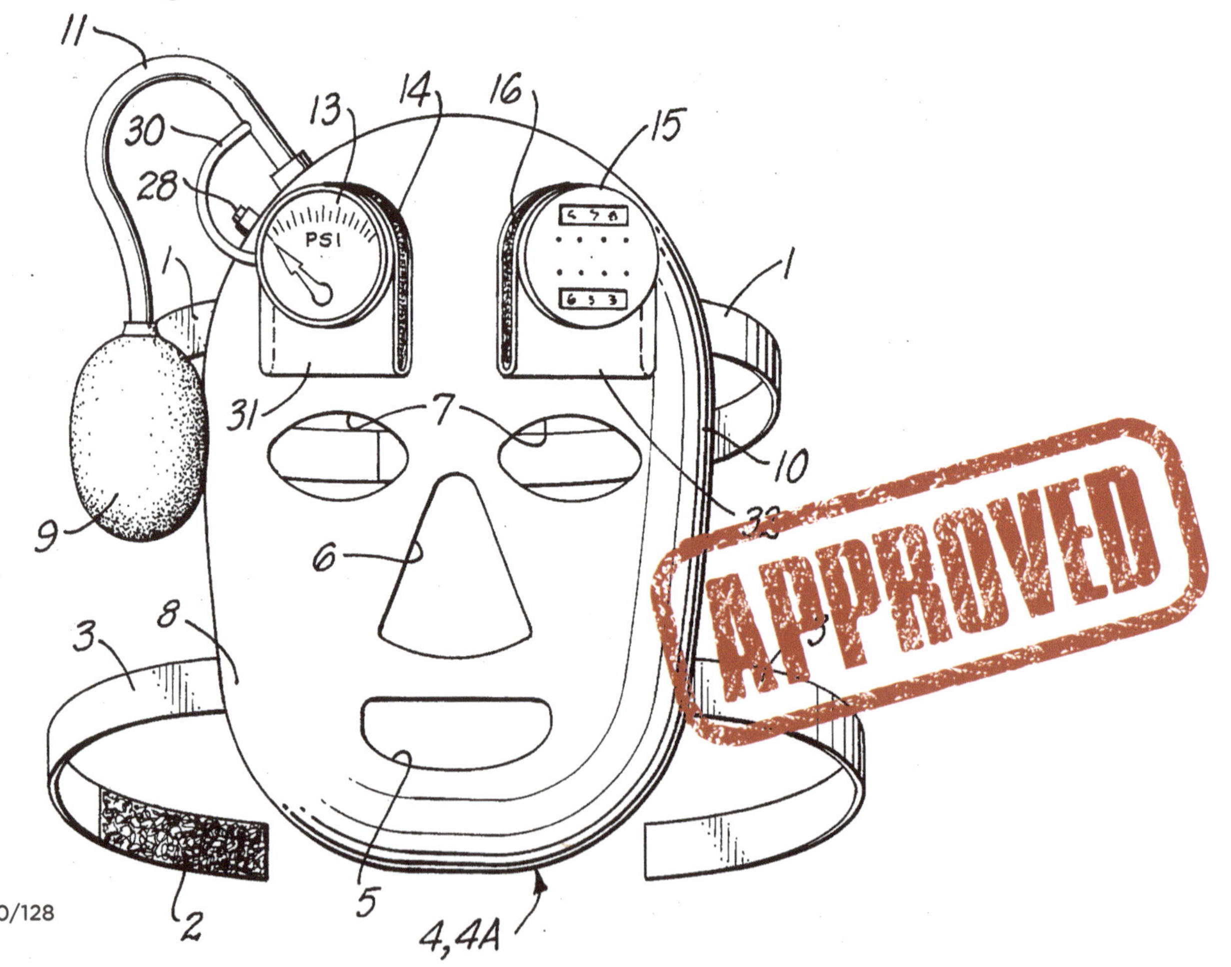

Terrorist Vehicle Arresting System

Gorlov, Alexander M., *Terrorist Vehicle Arresting System,* UNITED STATES PATENT Patent No. 4,759,655, Jul. 26, 1988.

A terrorist vehicle arresting system includes a crash barrier positioned at a side of a driveway instead of across the driveway; a gate across the entranceway which is dislodged by a vehicle coming through the closed gate; a net pulled out by the dislodged gate which captures the vehicle; a capstan to pivot a captured vehicle into the barrier; and cables from the net looped around the capstan, such that the netted vehicle is swung into the barrier where it comes to rest blocking the driveway. The impact-force is therefore redirected from the direction of the driveway, and the kinetic energy is dissipated upon impact with the offset, rigid barrier, thereby permitting the gate structure to be made light, aesthetically attractive, and quickly closed since the gate does not have to bear any substantial load.

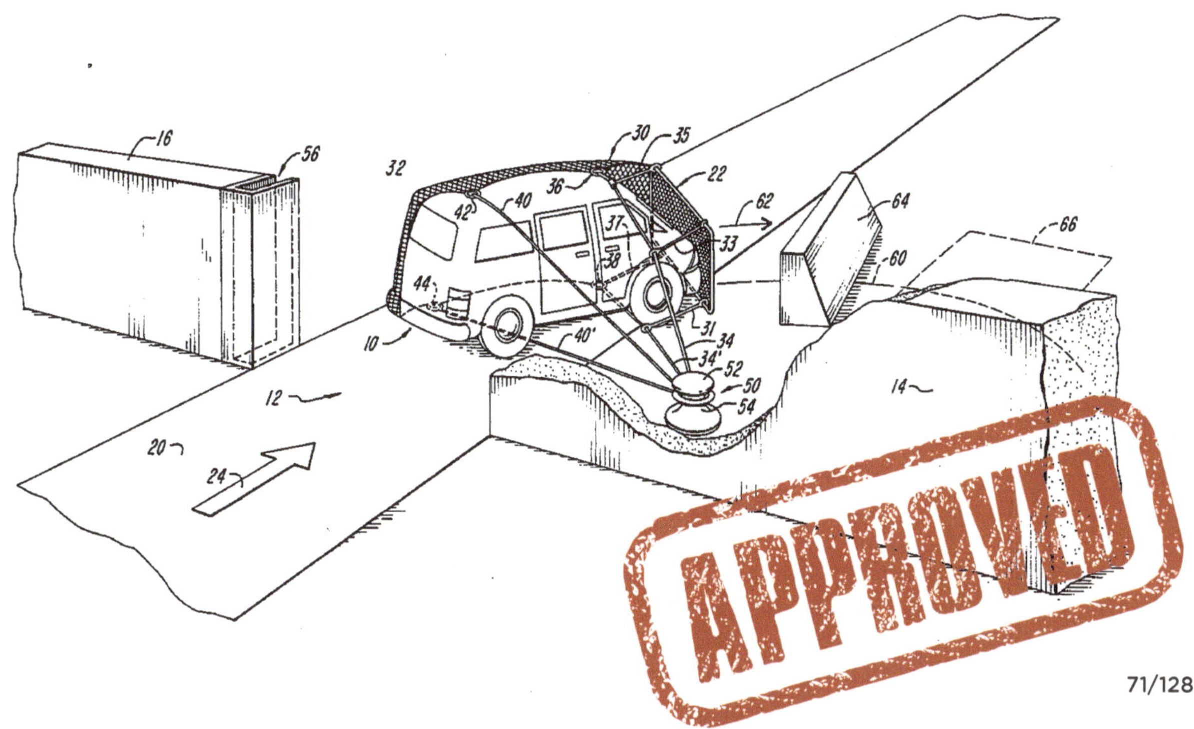

Apparatus for Molding Fruits in the Shape of Human Faces

Tweddell, Richard, *Method and Apparatus for Molding Fruits,* UNITED STATES PATENT Patent No. 4,827,666, May 9,1989.

A method and apparatus for growing squash, cucumbers and other fruits in desired shapes. The fruit, while growing on the plant, is enclosed within the internal cavity of an oversized mold having a cavity (inside) surface configured to form the desired details on the fruit. As growth continues the fruit fills the cavity and in doing so conforms with remarkable fidelity to the internal details of the mold. The mold is yieldable so as to allow the fruit to continue to expand outwardly after it has grown against the mold. The mold can be opened or removed after the fruit has conformed to its details, and the fruit is removed from the plant. The fruit can be eaten or, if dried, can provide a long-lasting sculptural item.

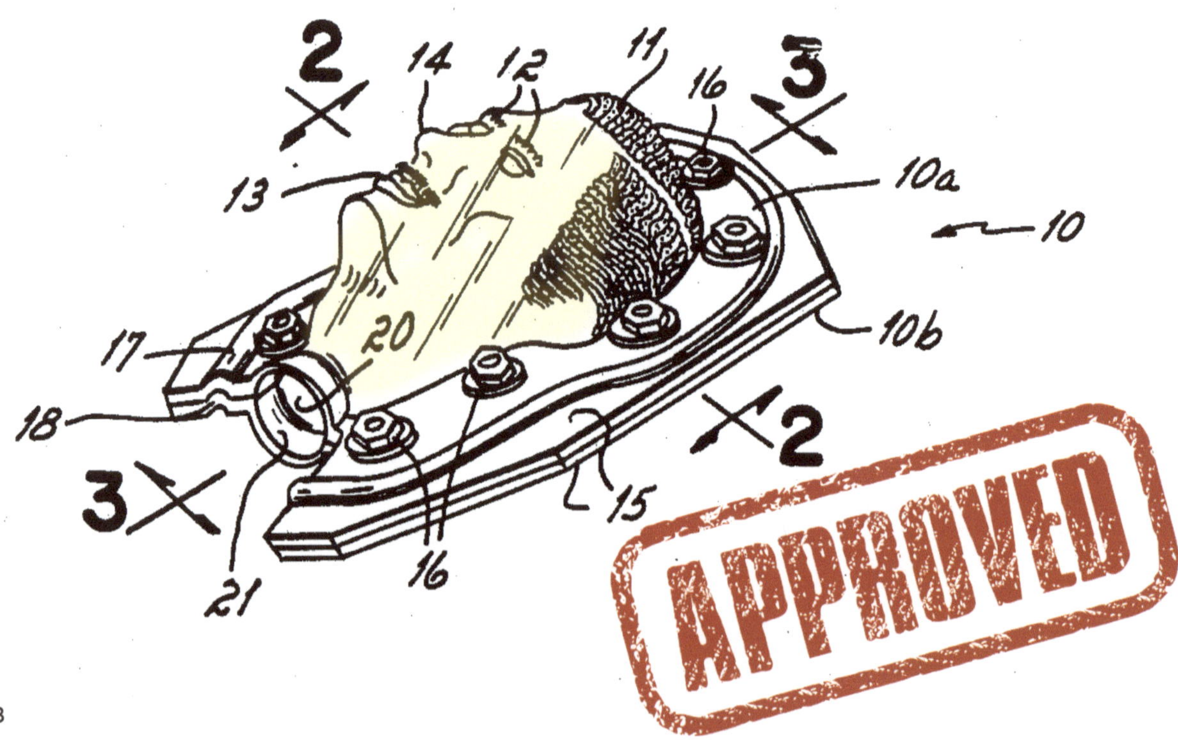

Shark Protector Suit

Fox, Nelson C. and Rosetta H. V. G., *Shark Protector Suit,* UNITED STATES PATENT Patent No. 4,833,729, May 30, 1989.

A shark protector suit of the invention is a combined rubber suit and helmet to completely cover the body of the wearer, including a face mask for facial protection, and preferably having at least a partial lining of flotation material, such as foam sheet. The suit and helmet have a plurality of spikes extending outward therefrom to prevent a shark from clamping its jaws over the wearer.

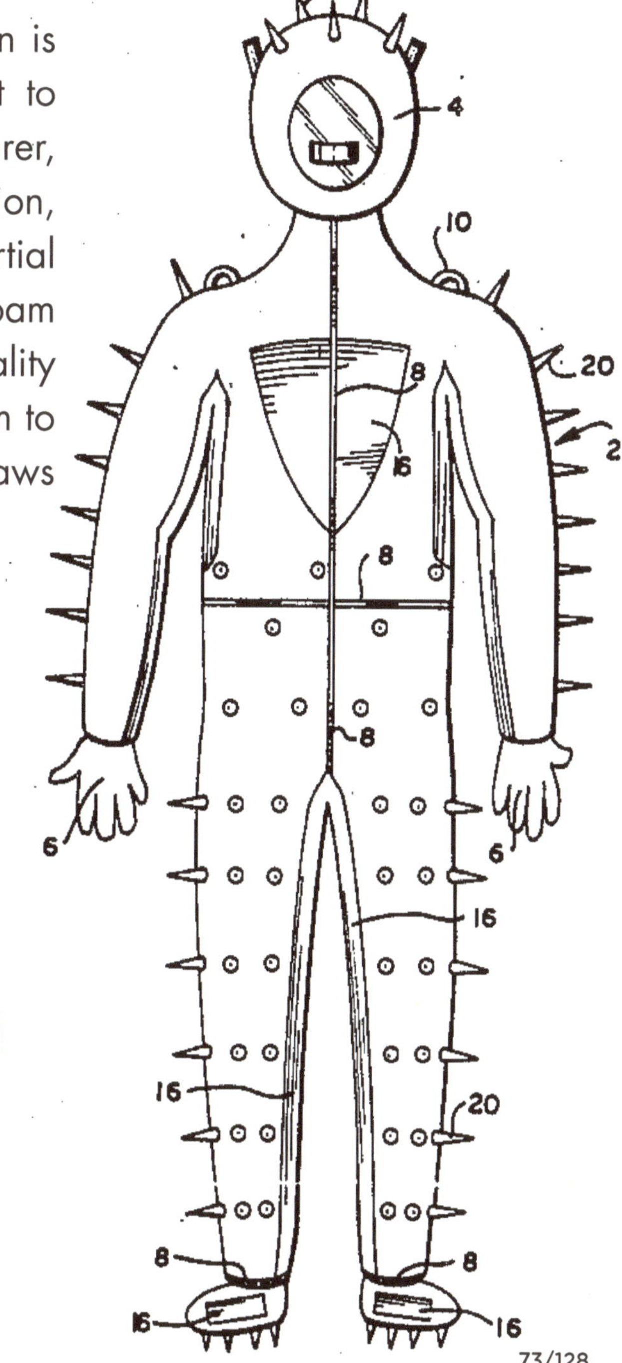

Novelty Moose Antlers Sun Glasses

Saccone, Louis V., *Novelty Sun Glasses With Information Display Having The Form Of Moose Antlers*, UNITED STATES PATENT Patent No. 4,909,620, Mar. 20, 1990.

This invention is a novelty head gear for wear by an individual and includes a pair of sunglasses having a novelty design of moose antlers attached to the sunglasses and extending sidewardly into opposite directions.

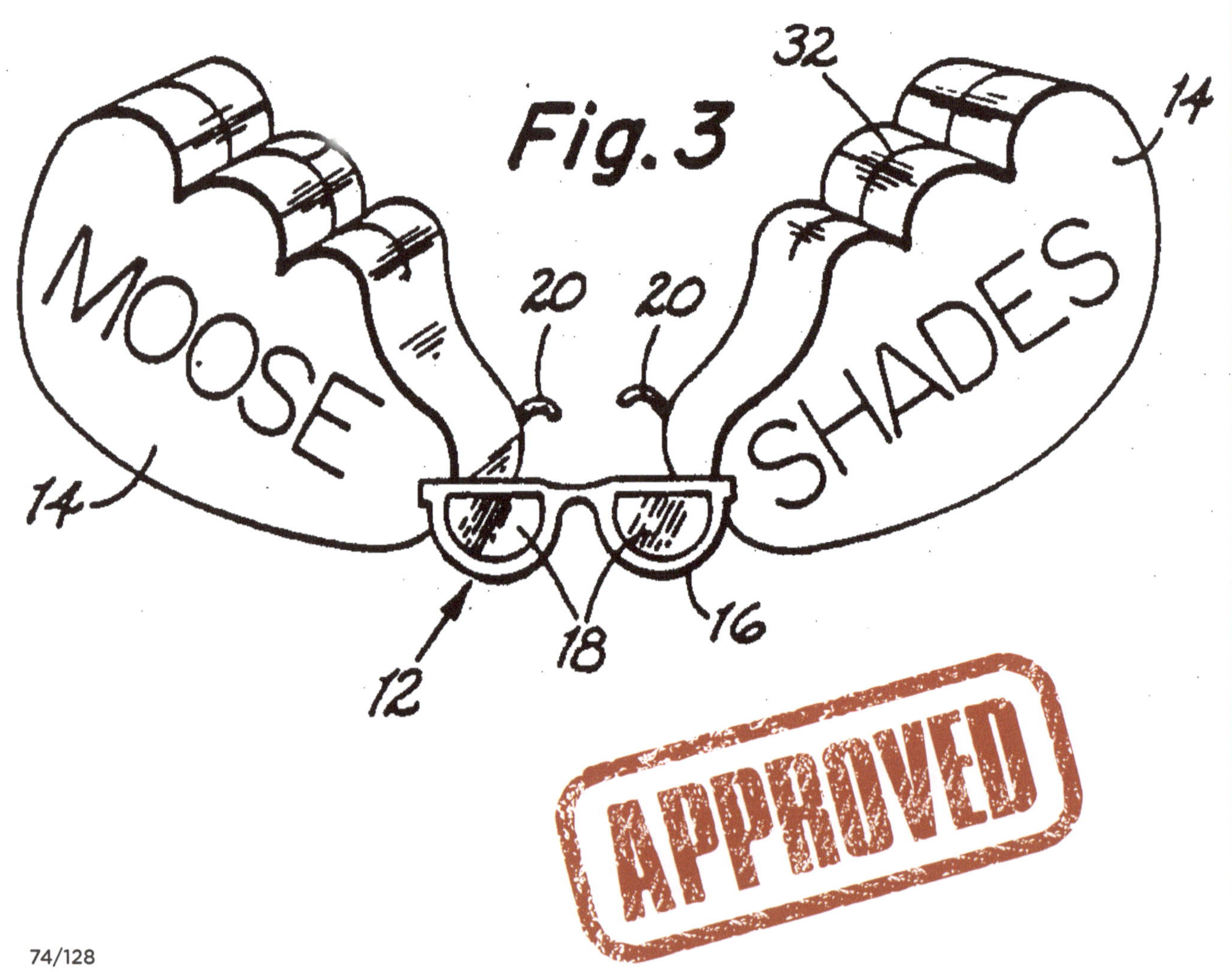

Clock for Keeping Time at a Rate other than Human Time

Metts, Rodney H., Thomas, Barry D., *Clock for Keeping Time at a Rate other than Human Time*, UNITED STATES PATENT Patent No. 5,023,850, Jun. 11, 1991.

A novelty clock, watch, and the like for keeping time at an animal's rate, defined in terms of a multiple of human rate by dividing the average lifetime of a particular animal into the average lifetime of a human being. The multiple for dogs is seven, for example. The device comprises a housing, a source of reference frequency for producing pulses, means for producing 60 pulses per second times the multiple for the particular animal, means for accumulating time, and means for displaying time. The display is the usual clock face with the speed of the hands altered, preferably also with the data indicated as the number of days since the last "new year" in animal days. A digital display of time in human terms may be provided with an analog display of time in animal terms or, alternatively, a capability to switch from one to the other may be provided. Preferably, a variable resistor, between the frequency source and producing means allows the user to change the multiple for different types of animals.

Fig. 1

Safety Walking Cane

Spaeth, Phillip A., *Safety Walking Cane,* UNITED STATES PATENT Patent No. 5,056,545, Oct. 15, 1991

An apparatus setting forth a walking cane provided with requisite safety features defined by an elongate cane shaft formed with a lowermost friction tip at its lower terminal end and a handle at its upper terminal end, with safety wheels mounted adjacent a lower terminal end, with lower surfaces of the safety wheels aligned with the lower tip. A light reflector is provided on the shaft and positioned medially between the spaced wheels and oriented forwardly thereof, and further including a water supply reservoir removably mounted relative to the shaft, a mirror, and a horn member, as well as an audible play-back device to alert others as to the positioning of the shaft in use.

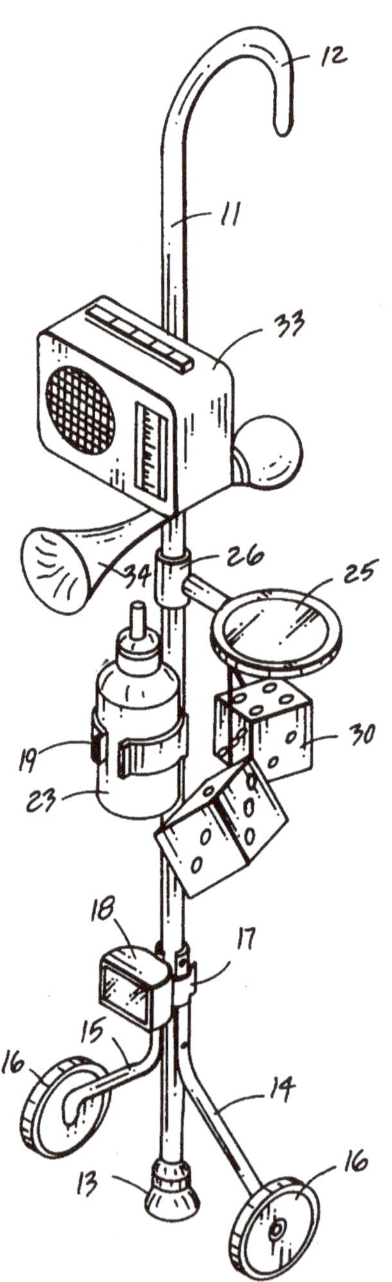

Helium-Filled Sun Shades

Sevilla, Frederick J., *Helium-Filled Sun Shades*, UNITED STATES PATENT Patent No. 5,076,029, Dec. 31, 1991.

A sun shade is formed from two sheets of a tough, yet flexible material which have been cut to an appropriate shape and size, and sealed together at the edges to form a flat, balloon-like structure. A plurality of interconnecting flow channels or buoyant cells are stitched into the sheets to enable the structure to retain its shape without bulging. A conventional fill valve is provided for filling the space between the sheets with helium or another suitable gas. The shade is anchored above a selected surface using cables or other flexible connectors.

Dog Umbrella

Celess, A., *Dog Umbrella*, UNITED STATES PATENT OFFICE Patent No. Des. 324,117, February 18, 1992.

The ornamental design for a dog umbrella, as shown and described.

DESCRIPTION
A perspective view of a dog umbrella showing design, it being understood that the broken lines are for illustrative purposes only and form no part of the claimed design.

Pistol-Shaped Pepper Grinder

Yang, Hang-Te, *Pistol-Shaped Pepper Grinder*, UNITED STATES PATENT Patent No. 5,199,655, Apr. 6,1993.

A pistol-shaped pepper grinder having a grinding plate and a grinding block provided inside a pistol-shaped housing, the grinding plate able to be moved by a trigger to grind pepper stored in a chamber on the grinding plate and going through the space between the grinding plate and the grinding block, the grinding block being able to be moved down so as to adjust the minuteness of the ground pepper, and ground pepper coming out of an exit provided in the right end of the housing.

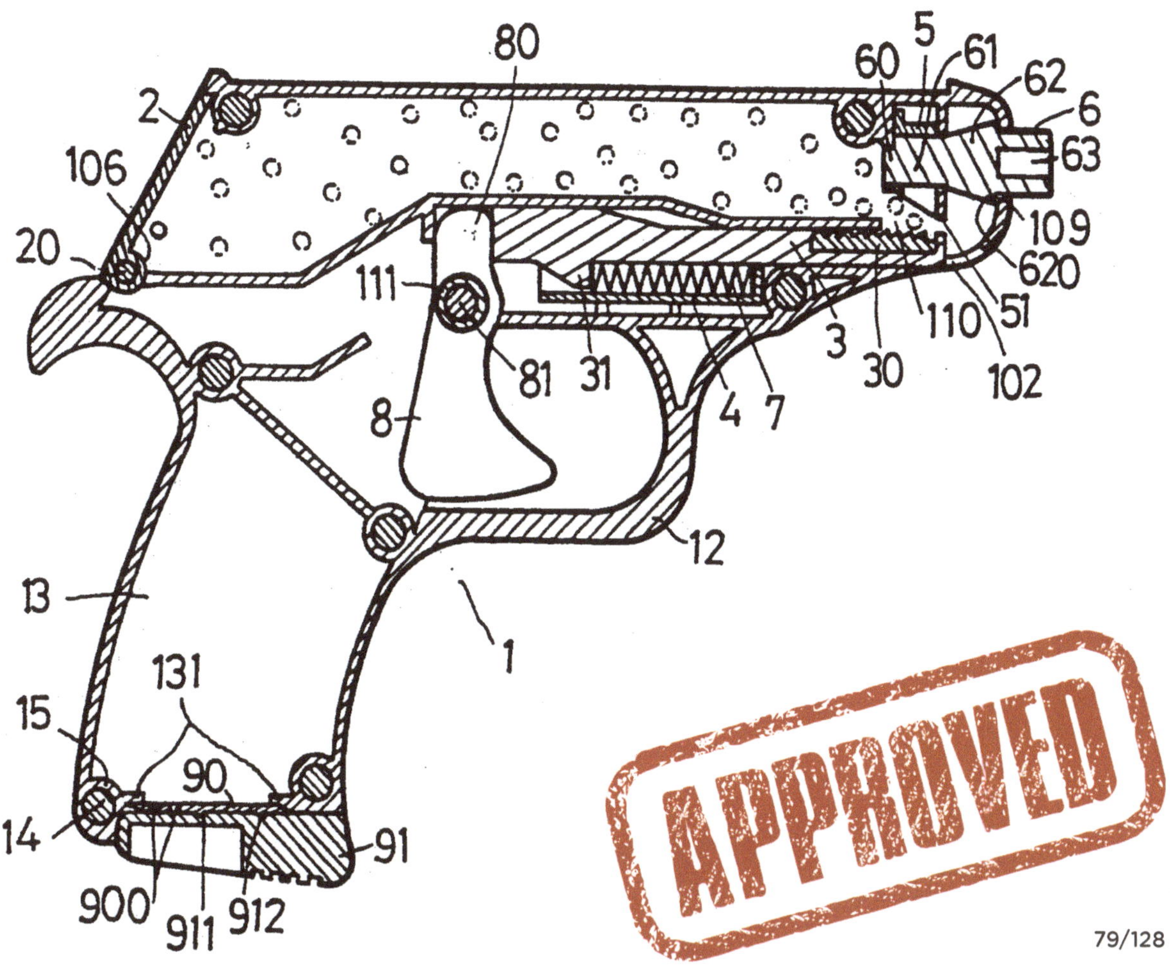

Barrier Device for Children

Frischmann, Thomas G., *Barrier Device for Children*, UNITED STATES PATENT Patent No. 5,255,958, Oct. 26,1993.

A struggling barrier for children includes a semirigid wall for blocking struggling movements which is attached to a flexible sheet for receiving sitting body weight of children. The method of sitting on the flexible sheet transfers body weight force to the attached wall thereby causing the flexible and movable device to become a semirigid and difficult to move barrier device.

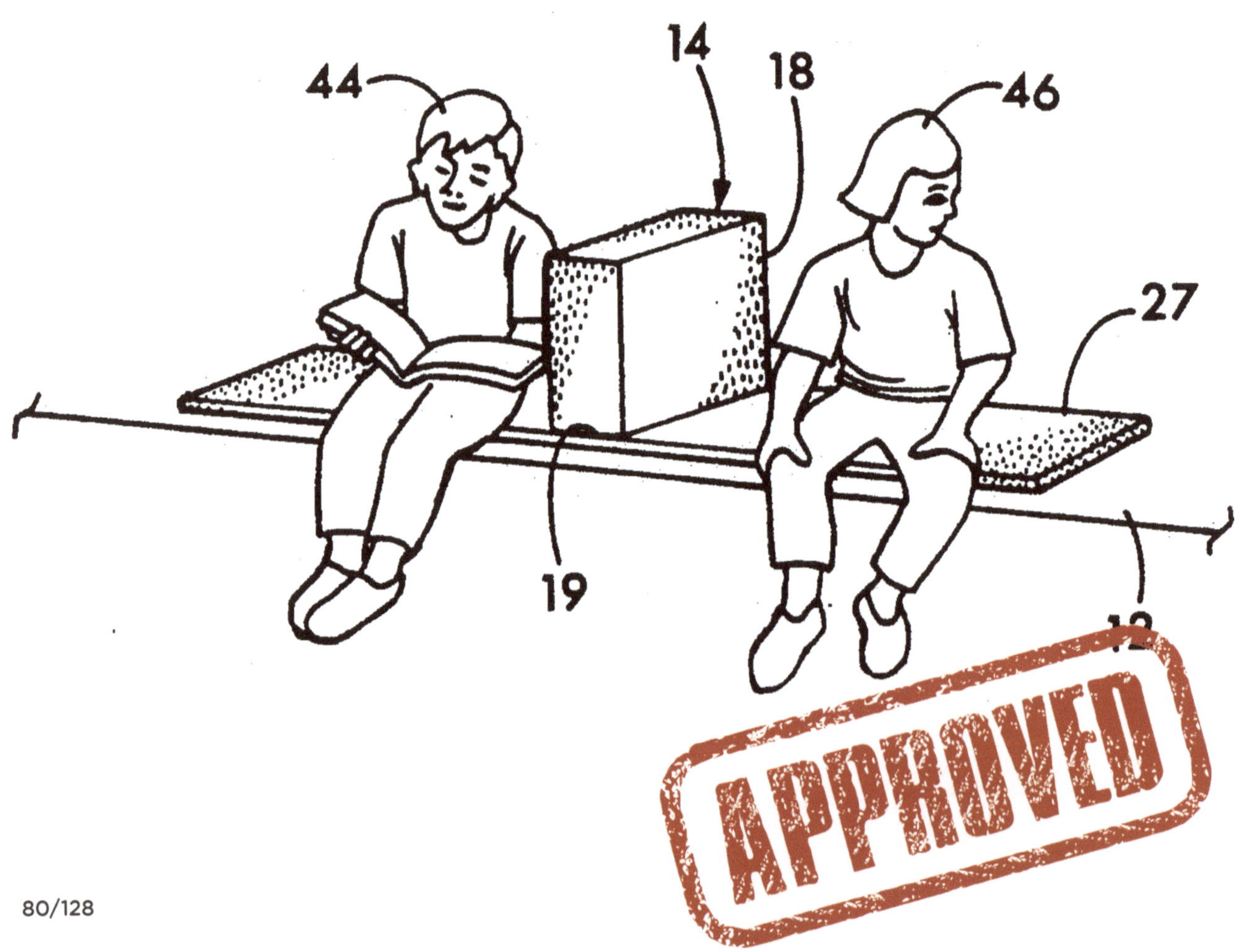

Apparatus for Simulating a "High-Five"

Cohen, Albert, *Apparatus for Simulating a "High-Five"*, UNITED STATES PATENT
Patent No. 5,356,330, Oct. 18,1994.

An apparatus for simulating a "high-five" including a lower arm portion
having a simulated hand removably attached thereto, an upper arm
portion, an elbow joint for pivotally securing the lower arm portion to the
upper arm portion, and a spring biasing element for biasing the upper
and lower arm portions towards a predetermined alignment.

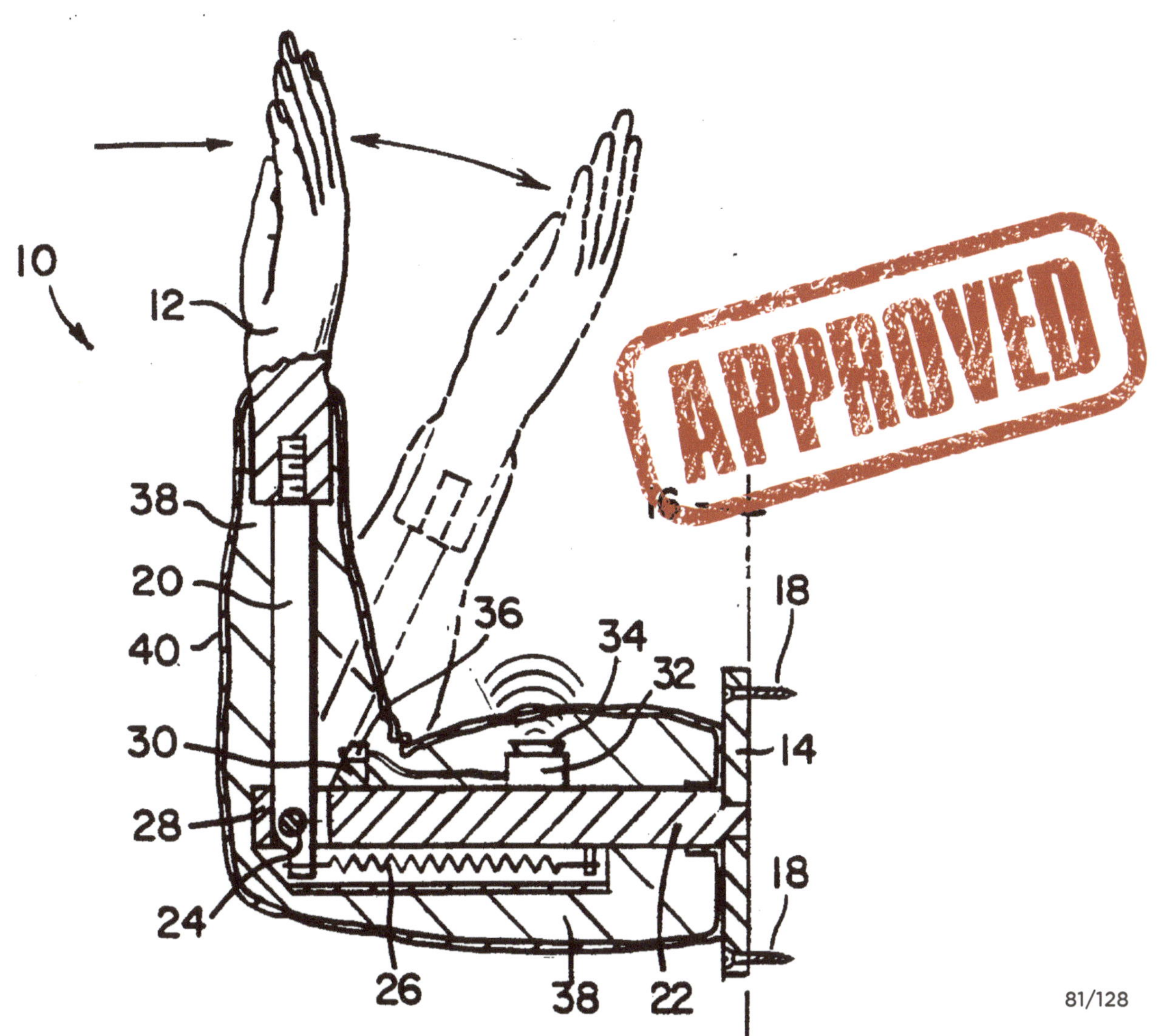

Method of Exercising a Cat

Amiss, Kevin T., Abbott, Martin H., *Method of Exercising a Cat*, UNITED STATES PATENT Patent No. 5,443,036, Aug. 22,1995.

A method for inducing cats to exercise consists of directing a beam of invisible light produced by a handheld laser apparatus onto the floor or wall or other opaque surface in the vicinity of the cat, then moving the laser so as to cause the bright pattern of light to move in an irregular way fascinating to cats, and to any other animal with a chase instinct.

Jaw, Face and Neck Muscle Exercise Apparatus

Miller, Warren G., *Jaw, Face and Neck Muscle Exercise Apparatus,* UNITED STATES PATENT Patent No. 5,501,646, Mar. 26, 1996.

A jaw and neck muscle exercise apparatus which includes a spring loaded support arm attached to a soft chin support on one end and to a chest plate on the other end. The chest plate is strapped around the chest bone/collar bone area and the back of the neck by a collar strap. The lower jaw may then be exercised by opening the mouth or lowering the entire head against the resistance of the spring. The resistance is selected to be proper for the size and strength of the user and the progress of the exercise program to date. Proper use of this device will cause the muscles of the face, chin and neck to become toned and conditioned, eliminating fatness below the chin and wrinkles, particularly exercising the hyoid, the infrahyoid and digastric muscles.

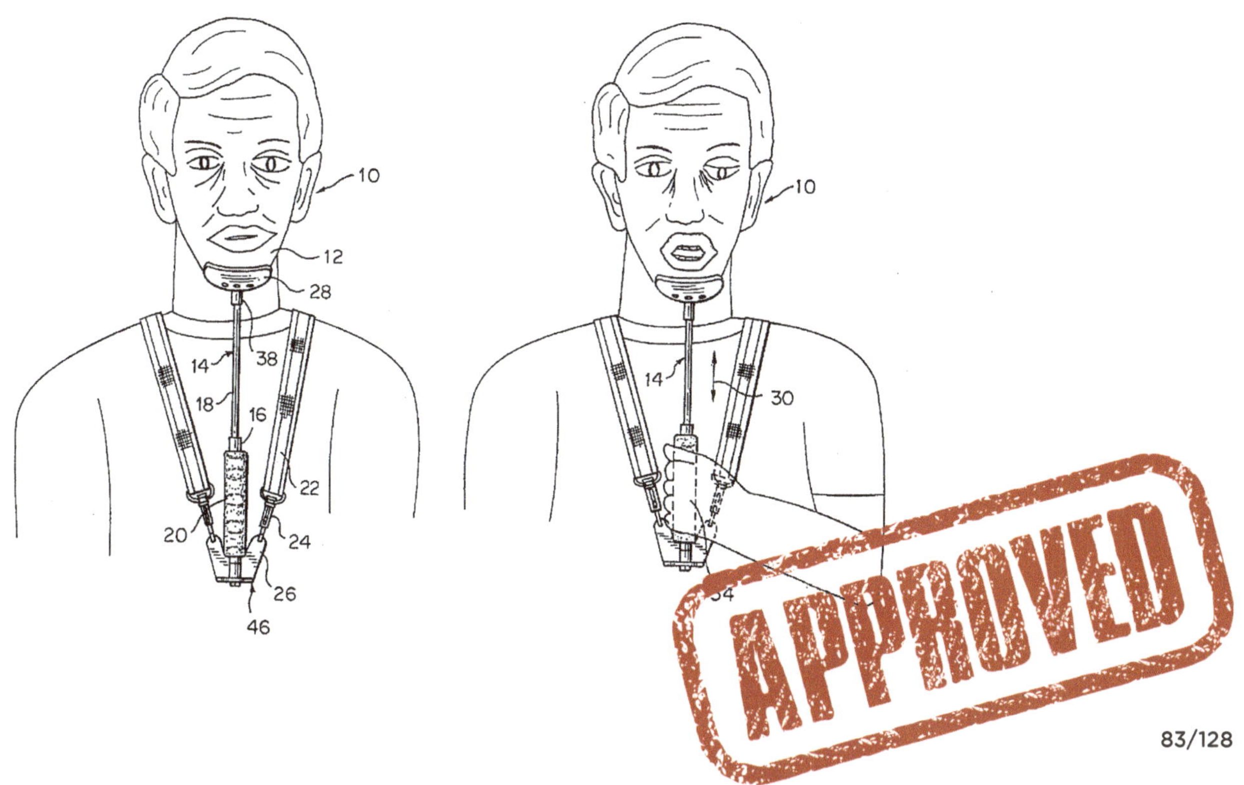

System for Removing a Vehicle Rider with a Parachute

Jackson, Troy, Leak, Joseph S. Sr., *Safety System for Removing a Rider from a Vehicle by Deploying a Parachute*, US PATENT Patent No. 5,593,111, Jan. 14, 1997.

Methods and apparatus for reducing the velocity of a rider in or on an open cockpit vehicle when the rider is thrown from the vehicle are disclosed. The present invention provides a drag-reducing device such as a parachute or parawing that is affixed to the rider so that when a crash occurs, the rider is slowed down after ejection and therefore more likely to survive the crash without severe injuries. The present invention is preferably used in conjunction with a motorcycle and includes a sensor system for sensing the imminence or occurrence of a crash an/or the ejection of the rider from the vehicle. A transmitter receiver system is used to relay a signal to a deployment system that is attached to the rider as part of a system containing the drag inducing device, which rapidly deployed, thereby causing the velocity of the ejected rider to be reduced and providing the further benefit of lifting the rider away from the crash site.

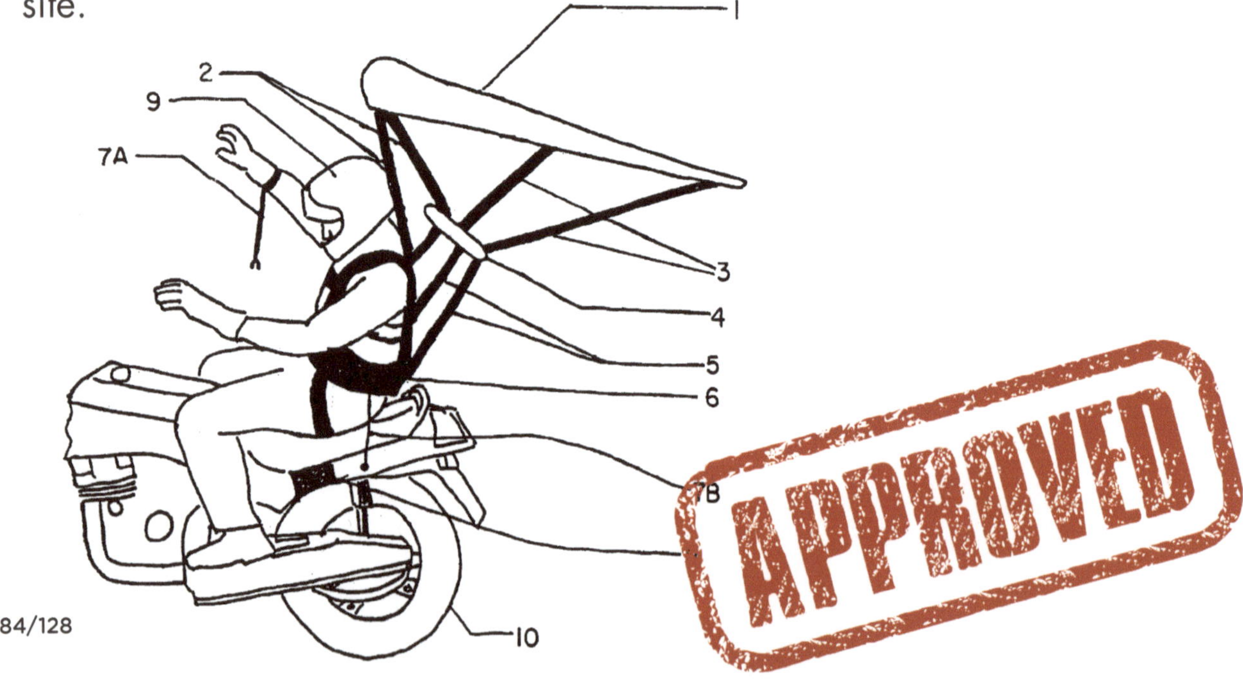

Graffiti Prevention Apparatus

Hunt, Jr., *Graffiti Prevention Apparatus*, UNITED STATES PATENT Patent No. 5,675318, Oct. 7, 1997

A system of components for preventing the application of graffiti to property includes one or more sensors and a signal transmitter at or near the surface to be defaced, and signal receiving means for actuating a mechanism in the spray apparatus or at the surface to be protected which will enable prevention of the surface targeted for defacement. One embodiment of the invention includes a signal receiver in the

spray canister which actuates an electromagnet to move a plug in the marking material delivery tube to a flow blocking position. A second embodiment of the invention includes a signal receiver in the spray canister coupled to a rotatable magnet for rotating the upper end of the delivery tube away from the spray nozzle thereby breaking the path through which the marking material travels from the spray apparatus to the target surface. A third embodiment of the invention provides for the creation of an electromagnetic field at the targeted surface, and the mixing of the marking material (either by the "paint" manufacturer or afterwards) with a magnetic material so that when sprayed at the surface, the marking material is repelled.

Pantyhose Garment with Spare Leg Portion

Pappas, Annette L., Vaccaro, Nita A., *Pantyhose Garment with Spare Leg Portion*, UNITED STATES PATENT Patent No. 5,713,081, Feb. 3, 1998.

A hosiery item including a panty member having three absorbent crotch members provided therein, each absorbent crotch member having a pocket formed therein; and three leg portions secured to the panty member in a manner such that an absorbent crotch member is positioned between any two leg portions, each leg portion having a leg insertion opening in connection with an interior of the panty member. In use the wearer inserts her legs into two of the leg opening in the conventional fashion of donning a pair of pantyhose. The remaining unused leg portion is then gathered and the toe end tucked into the pocket of one of the absorbent crotch members. If a run or hole develops in one of the leg portions being worn, the leg of the wearer can be easily and rapidly removed from the damaged leg portion and placed into the undamaged spare leg portion. The damaged leg portion is then gathered, folded and tucked into a pocket of one of the absorbent crotch members as wearer to select and use any two of the three leg portions for use.

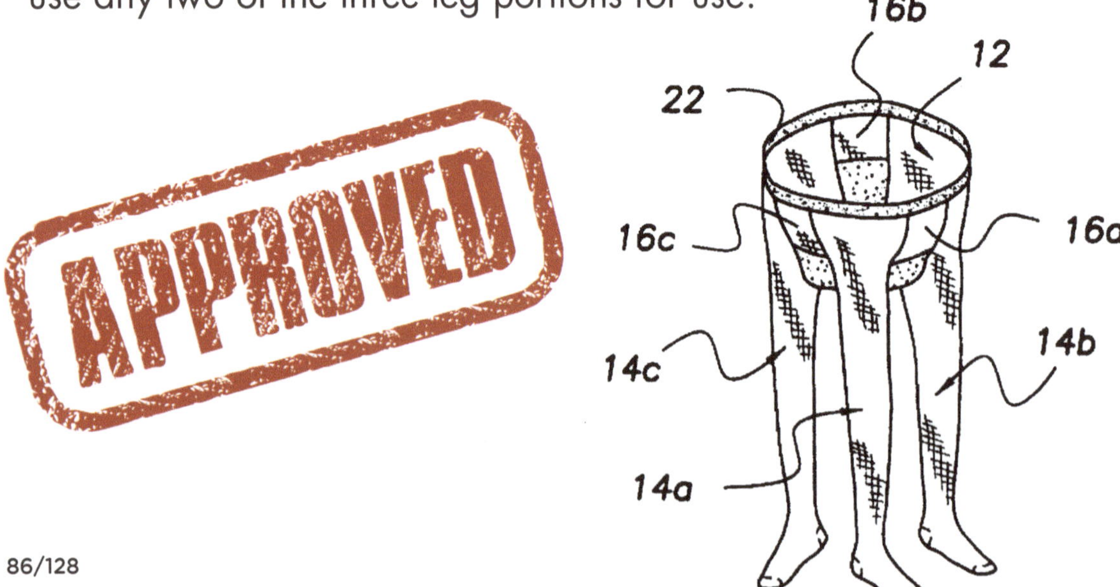

Kissing Shield

Wood, Deloris Gray, *Kissing Shield*, UNITED STATES PATENT Patent No. 5,727,565, Mar. 17, 1998.

A kissing shield comprised of a thin, flexible membrane and a frame or holder. The membrane is closed on three sides, a fourth side remaining open so that the membrane can be stretched over the frame or holder. The frame or holder consists of a supporting member and an elongated handle. The supporting member adapts over the bottom part of the user's face and has sufficient dimension to cover the lips and most of the cheeks and extends from under the nose to the bottom of the chin. The elongated handle extends laterally from the supporting member and is sized to be held in the hand of the user such that the hand is spaced apart from the supporting member and membrane. In use, the membrane is placed over the frame or holder. Using the handle potion of the frame or holder, the user places the kissing shield under his nose, so that it covers his lips, cheeks and chin. The user then positions the kissing shield between his lips and the lips or cheek of the individual he plans to kiss and kisses the intended recipient of his affection.

Fire Escape Parachute

Yu, Yu-Li, *Fire Escape Parachute,* UNITED STATES PATENT Patent No. 5,826,678, Oct. 27, 1998.

A fire escape parachute is provided and includes a center shaft, top ribs, stretcher ribs, a main runner, reinforcing ribs, an upper runner, a fabric and a safety belt. The function of the runner is to drive the stretcher ribs which in turn push the top ribs to open the fabric. The reinforcing ribs will tightly pull the outer ends of the top ribs, so that the top ribs are bent downwards to form an arc and such is secured by reinforcing ropes to effectively prevent reverse upward turning of the fabric and the top ribs. Thus, in case of fire in a high-rise building, the fabric can be controlled and opened directly by the escapee, who will use the fire escape parachute to slowly descend from the high-rise building.

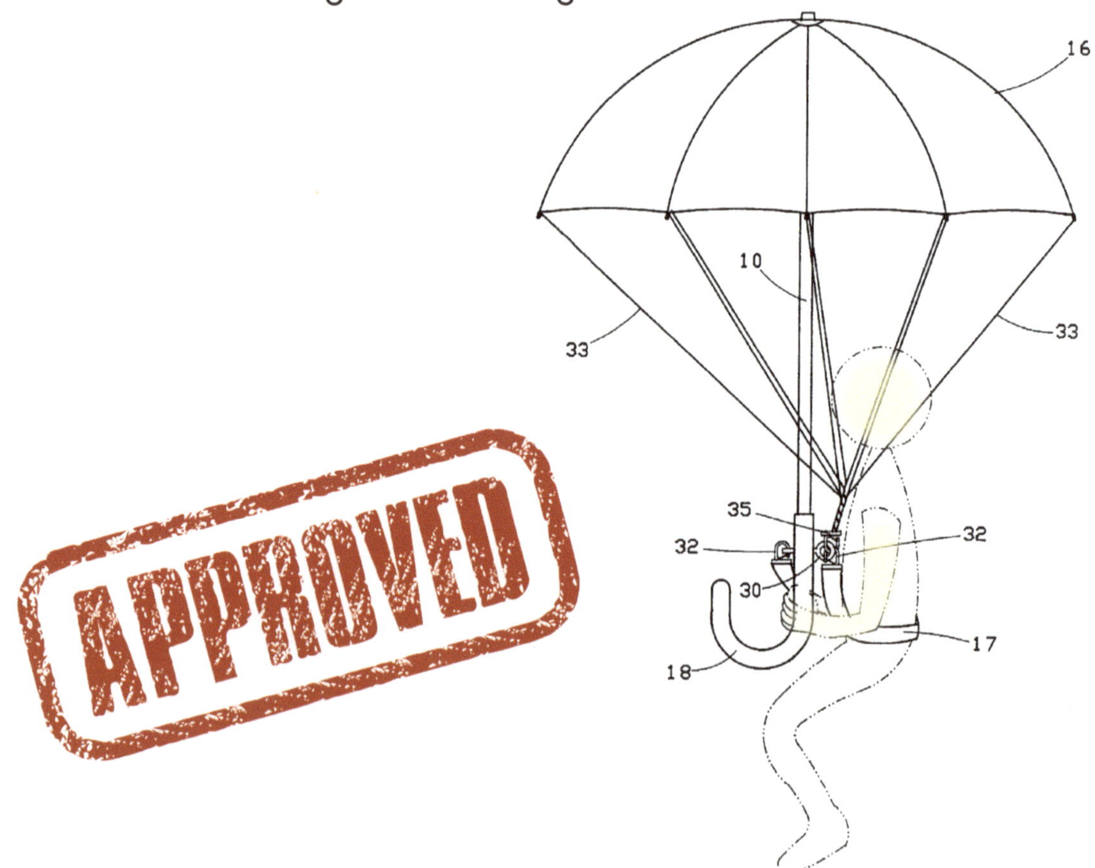

Toe Puppet

Budreck, David J., *Toe Puppet,* UNITED STATES PATENT Patent No. 5,830,035, Nov. 3, 1998.

A puppet is adapted to be mounted on a single human digit for providing animated motion of a figurine responsive to movement of the single human digit. The puppet comprises a hollow, elastic cap having an interior wall defining a cavity into which the single human digit is snugly received. The cap includes a resilient neck portion for supporting the figurine at a distance spaced from the single human digit such that movement of the single human digit causes the neck portion and the figurine to oscillate to and fro under the influence of the weight of the figurine.

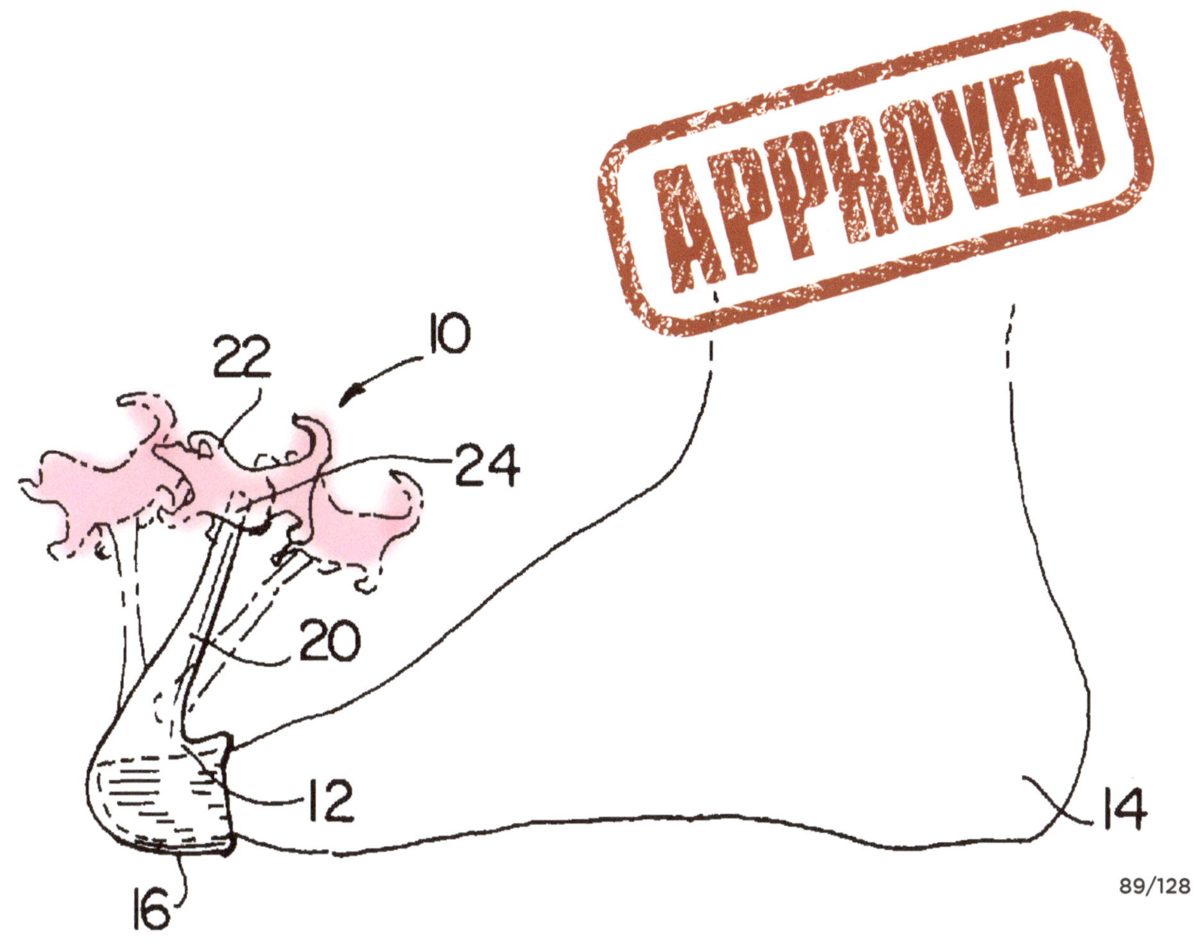

Pet Display Clothing

Belisle, Brice, *Pet Display Clothing,* UNITED STATES PATENT Patent No. 5,901,666, May 11,1999.

A vest or belt is integrally formed with tubular, pet receiving passageways which extend around the wearer's body and terminate in pocket-like chambers for feeding and retrieval. Outer wall portions ol the passageways are transparent so that a pet moving along the passageways can be seen by a spectator. Graphics or indicia depicting the pet's habitat or a pet story are marked on the vest and extend across portions ol the passageways masking delineations or depicting the passageways as burrows.

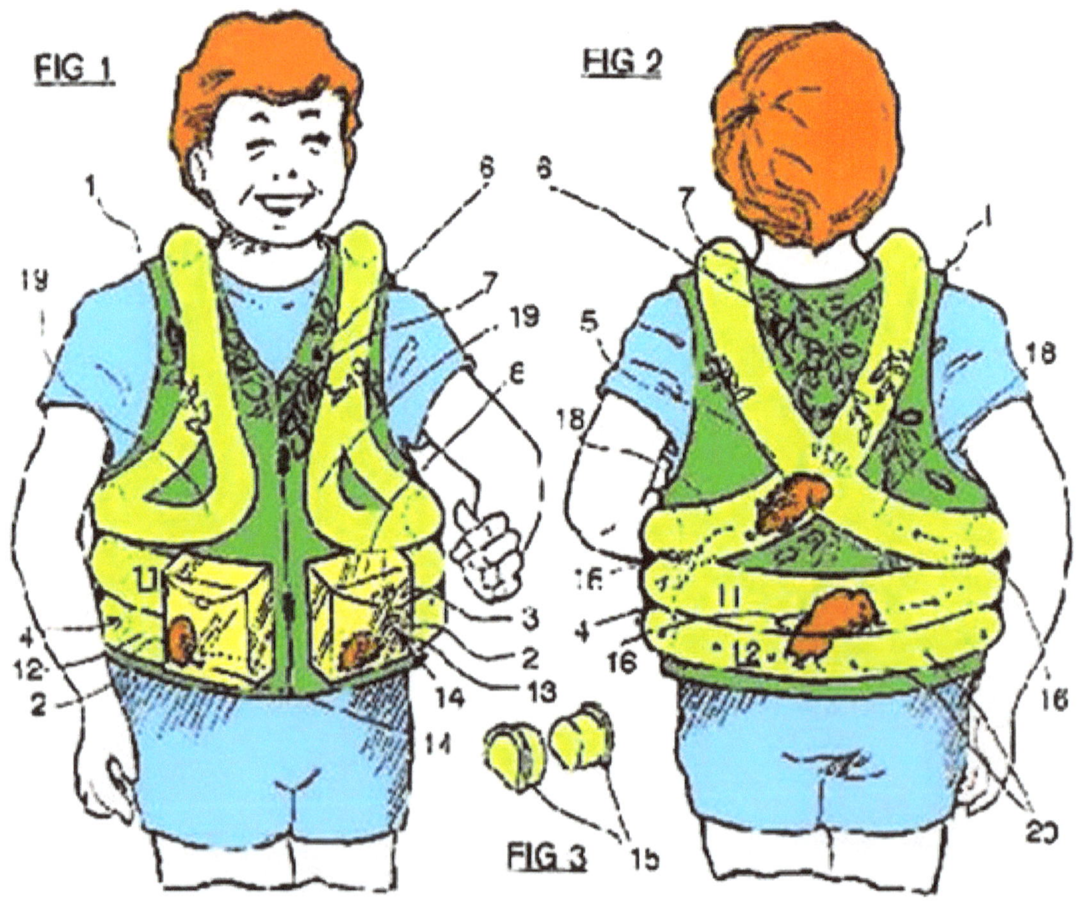

Armor with Rollers

Blondeau, Jean-Yves, *Armor with Rollers*, UNITED STATES PATENT Patent No. 5,926,857, Jul. 27,1999.

An armor with rollers is provided that enables a user to move in all positions by rolling on a hard and smooth surface while constantly varying his bearing points on the ground. The armor includes a pair of gauntlets extending from beyond the user's hand to the user's elbow and having rollers at both ends thereof. The armor also includes a pair of rigid leg pads having rollers near the user's knees.

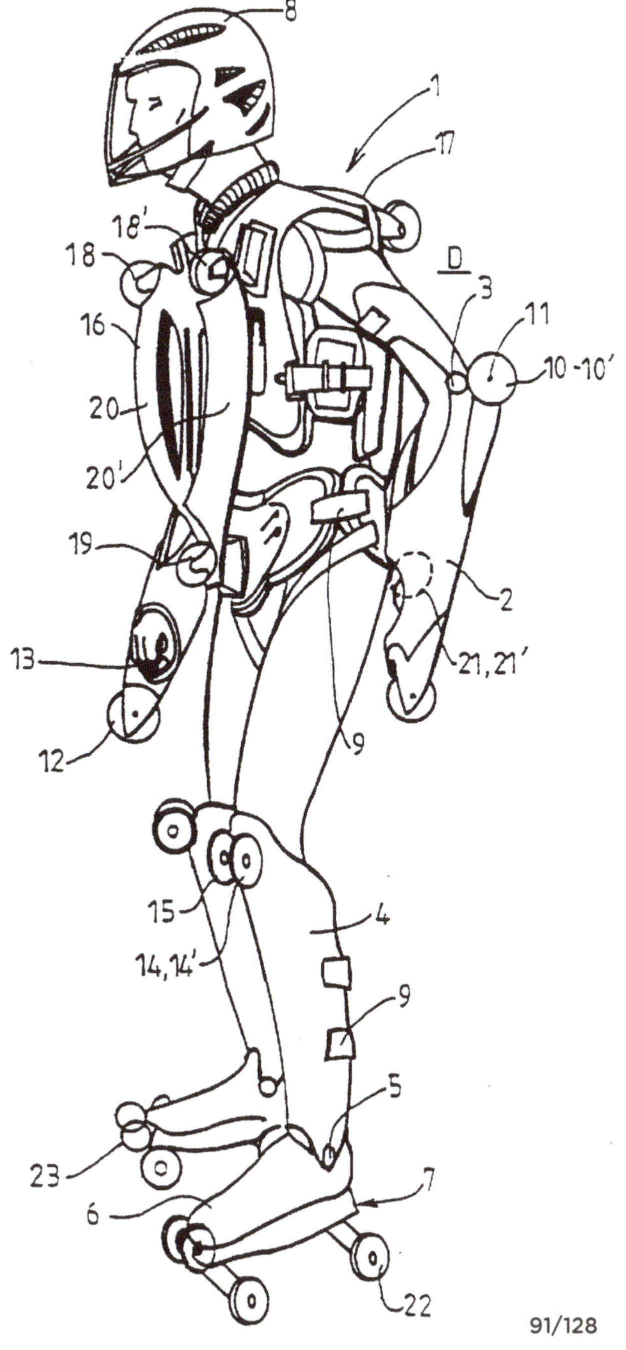

Substance Dispensing Headgear

Flann, Randall D., *Substance Dispensing Headgear,* UNITED STATES PATENT Patent No. 5,966,743, Oct. 19,1999.

A headgear for dispensing a substance has a container to carry the substance. A spigot is secured to the container. The spigot can be opened to dispense the substance by gravity, suction, pressure or levity flow when the container. The spigot can be closed to retain the substance in the chamber. A hat-like recess is formed within the bottom wall ol the container sized for wearing on an individual's head, and for maintaining the container in a freestanding condition during hands-free ambulation ol the individual.

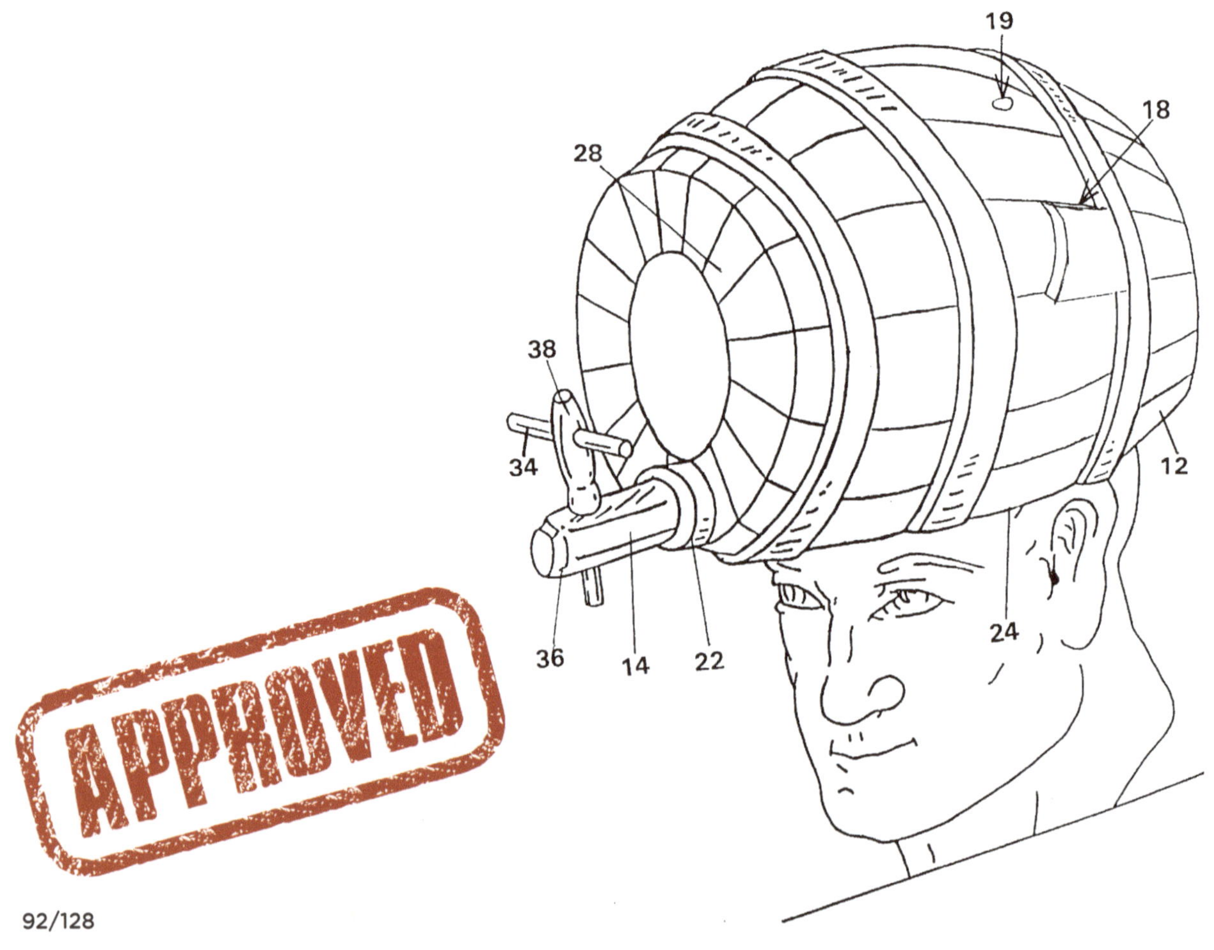

Motorized Ice Cream Cone

Hartman, Richard B., *Motorized Ice Cream Cone*, UNITED STATES PATENT Patent No. 5,971,829, Oct. 26,1999.

A novelty amusement eating receptacle for supporting, rotating and sculpting a portion ol ice cream or similarly malleable food while it is being consumed comprising: a handheld housing, a cup rotatably supported by the hand-held housing and adapted to receive and contain a portion ol ice cream or food product ol similar consistency, and a drive mechanism in the hand-held housing for imparting rotation upon the cup and rotationally feeding its contents against a person's outstretched tongue.

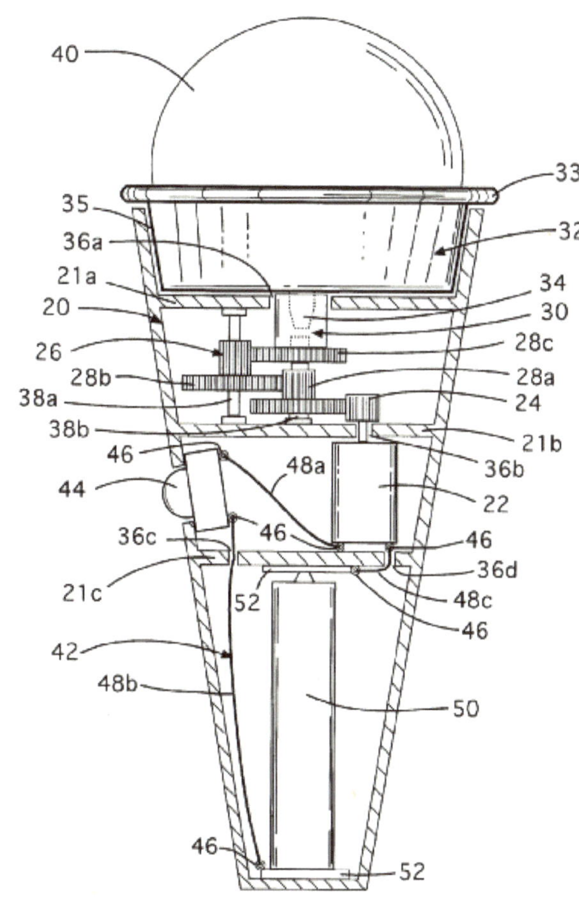

Wearable Device for Feeding and observing Birds

Leslie, David M., *Wearable Device for Feeding and observing Birds*, UNITED STATES PATENT Patent No. 5,996,127, Dec. 7,1999.

A device for feeding and observing flying animals comprising a hat, a support mounted on the hat and extending outward from the hat, and a feeder mounted on the support. When flying animals feed from the feeders, a person wearing the hat may observe them from a short distance. The device may comprise a helmet with three poles mounted on it and extending outward from the helmet, and a feeder hanging from each ol the poles. A variety ol flying animals, including butterflies, hummingbirds, and other small birds, may be observed with the device.

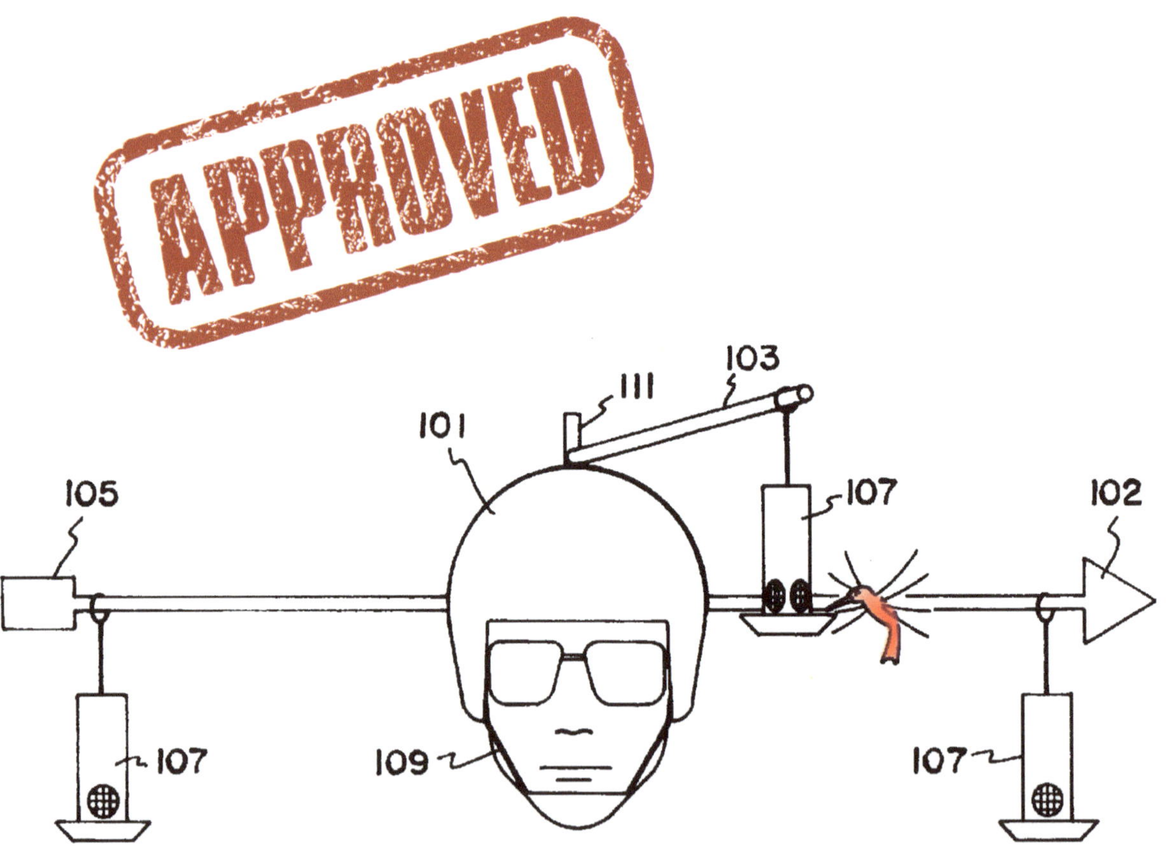

User Support Device

Green, William Adam, *User Support Device,* UNITED STATES PATENT Patent No. 6,126,180, Oct. 3,2000.

A user support device which provides an alternative to a conventional chair or seat is described. The device supports the user in an inclined position. The device has a first portion for supporting a front torso area and a front thigh area of the user and a second portion for supporting a front knee area and a front shin area ol the user. A frame connects the first portion and the second portion. The invention provides a method for positioning a user to operate equipment. The method is carried out by positioning the user's torso front in a torso front down, forward lacing position to operate the equipment on a torso-supporting first area ol a first portion of an elongated platform.

Bubbling Brain Novelty

Thomas Carl Weber, *Bubbling Brain Novelty*, UNITED STATES PATENT Patent No. 6,193,578 Bl, Feb. 27, 2001.

A transparent vessel containing a fluid and a life-like full scale human brain inserted into the fluid is used for novelty purposes. The vessel is open on its top and sealed on its bottom, and is mounted on a base portion of the device. Air bubbles are produced from an air pump attached to the side of the base portion. A tube connected to the air pump and an outlet port is positioned inside of the vessel, immersed in the liquid to supply air. The transparent, water-tight brain vessel is lit from underneath by a lamp. To enhance an effect of a scientific fiction experiment, the novelty is placed on a stand and has one or more decorative perforated tubes attached for visual effect. The tank is preferably covered with a dome-shaped lid.

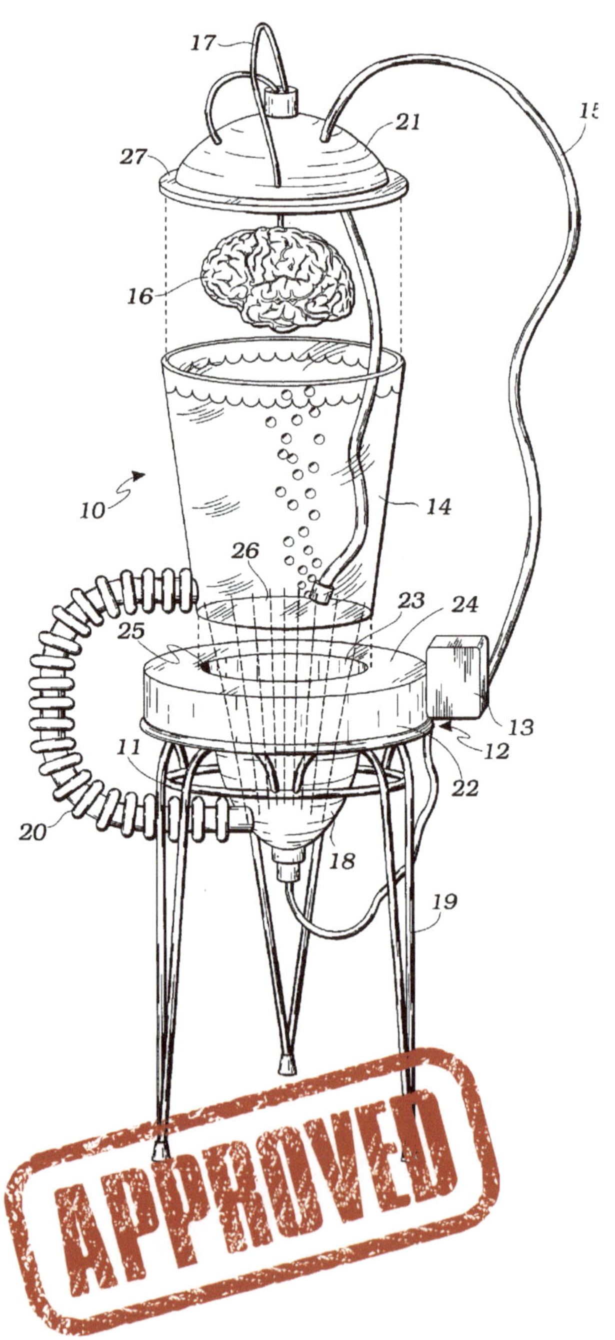

"

Cycling Activity Belt

Norton, Laurie J., *Cycling Activity Belt*, UNITED STATES PATENT Patent No. 6,224,450 Bl, May 1, 2001.

An activity belt to be worn by a cyclist has amusement devices attached. The amusement devices entertain a child riding in a child carrier seat behind the cyclist. The amusement devices may attach with clips so they can be changed to suit the age and interests of the child. The activity belt provides back support for the cyclist and a pocket for storing small items while cycling.

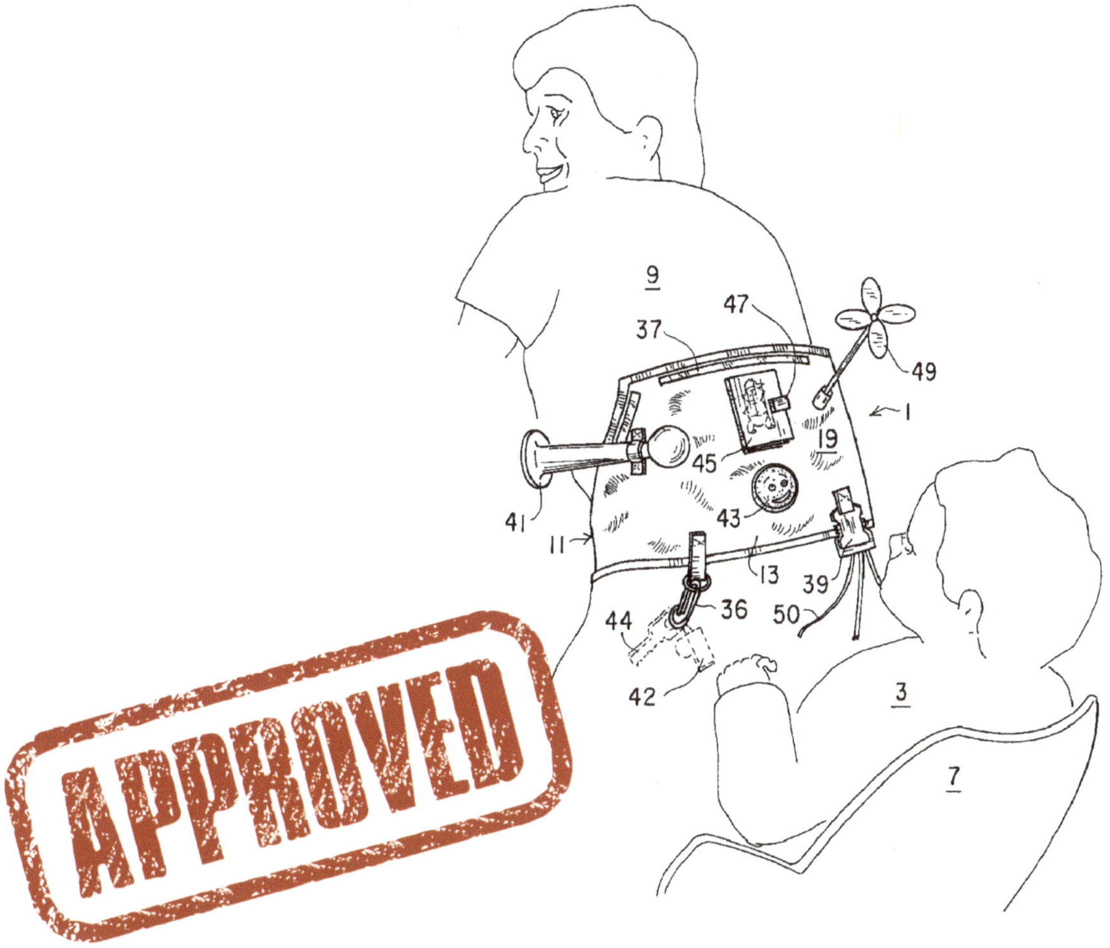

Snake Repellent System

Pogue, Thelma F., *Snake Repellent System,* UNITED STATES PATENT Patent No. 6,244,518 Bl, Jun. 12, 2001.

A snake repellent system for use in repelling snakes so as to prevent the human user from being bitten. The snake repellent system consists of a receptacle into which is placed a quantity of garlic or onion, the aroma of which is believed to be effective in repelling snakes. The receptacle is provided with a lid having a plurality of openings for facilitating the dispersal of the garlic or onion aroma. The receptacle may be provided with a mincing rack used to mince a clove of garlic, thereby more fully releasing its aroma. The receptacle may also be provided with a means to both limit child access to the repellent substance within the receptacle and prevent removal of the repellent substance from the lid openings. An adjustable band is provided for attaching the receptacle to the arm or leg of the user.

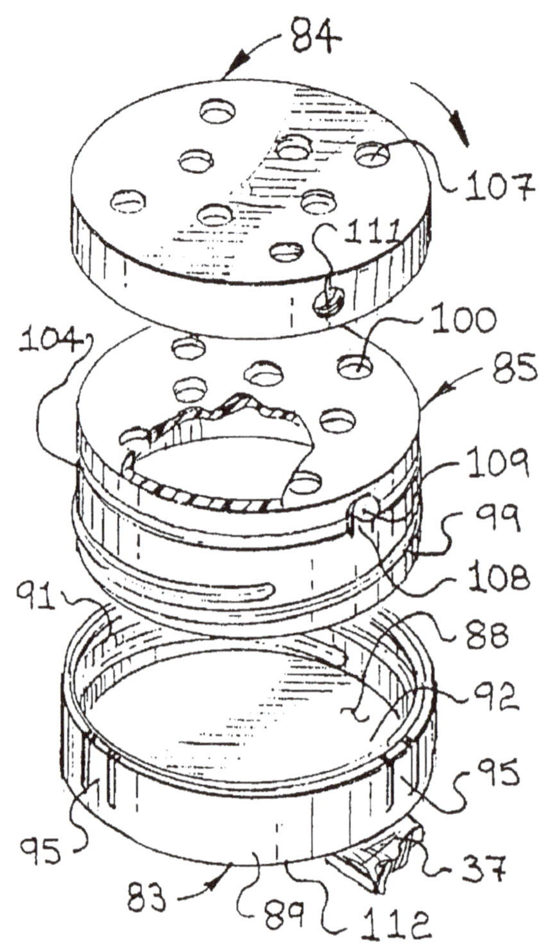

Brassiere with integrated bladder for drinking liquids

Shailer, Tracy B., *Brassiere with integrated bladder for drinking liquids*, UNITED STATES PATENT Patent No. 6,241,575 Bl, Jun. 5, 2001.

Cups of a bra include integrated flexible bladders formed of a medical grade material having sufficient fluid integrity to hold a comestible liquid. Each bladder is provided with an inlet, for purposes of filling, and an outlet for purposes of consumption. The bladder inlet is typically located at a portion of the bladder facing closest to the vertical axis of the body, while the outlet is advantageously positioned at the lowestmost point of the bladder to gain the fullest benefit of gravity on fluid flow through the outlet tube which, during periods of non-use, may be hidden in a number of ways, these including wrapping about the periphery of the bra cup itself, placing the tube underneath a bra strap, and placing the tube along the back of the user where one is wearing an article of clothing, such as a blouse, tank top, or bikini top which will hide such tube.

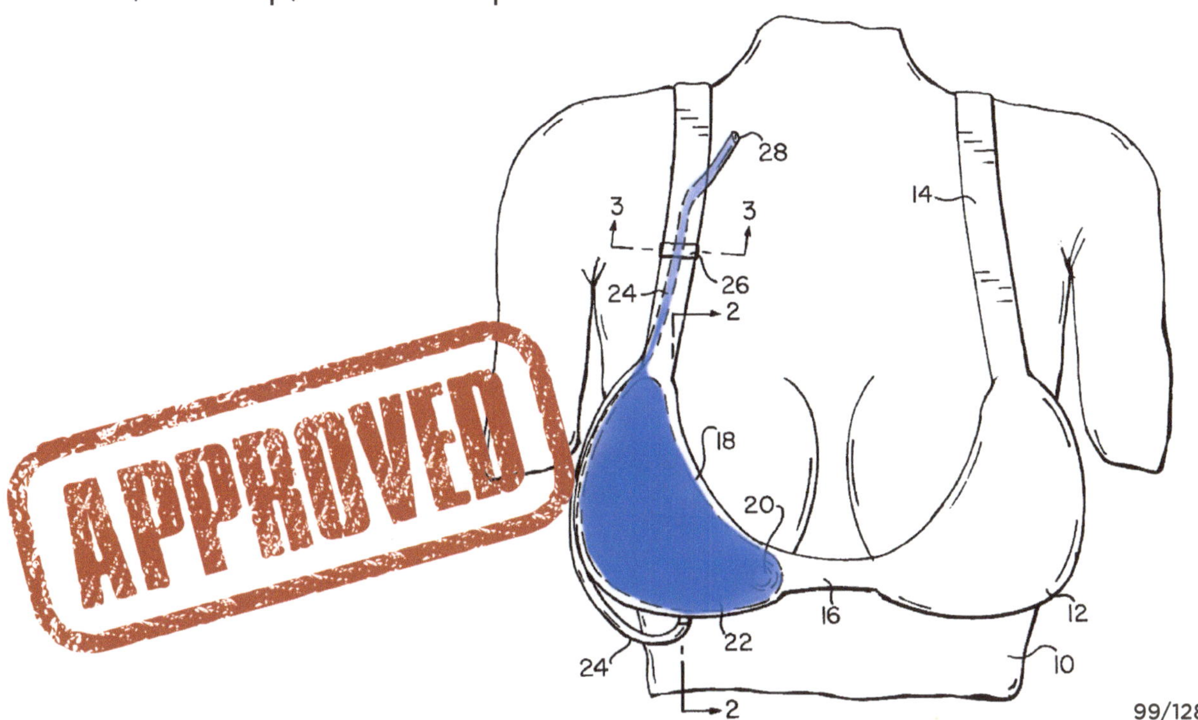

Aquatic Propulsion Device

Brown, William B., *Aquatic Propulsion Device*, UNITED STATES PATENT Patent No. 6,264,519 Bl, Jul. 24, 2001.

An aquatic propulsion device is provided comprising a harness to be worn on the body of a person, at least a first elongate member, and at least a first paddle. The first elongated member has first and second opposed ends and a first grip. The first end is pivotally securable to the harness. The first paddle is secured to the second end of the first elongated member. The first grip is positioned so that a person, when wearing the harness, can reach and hold onto the grip with a first hand and move the first grip so that the first elongated member and the first paddle pivot relative to the harness.

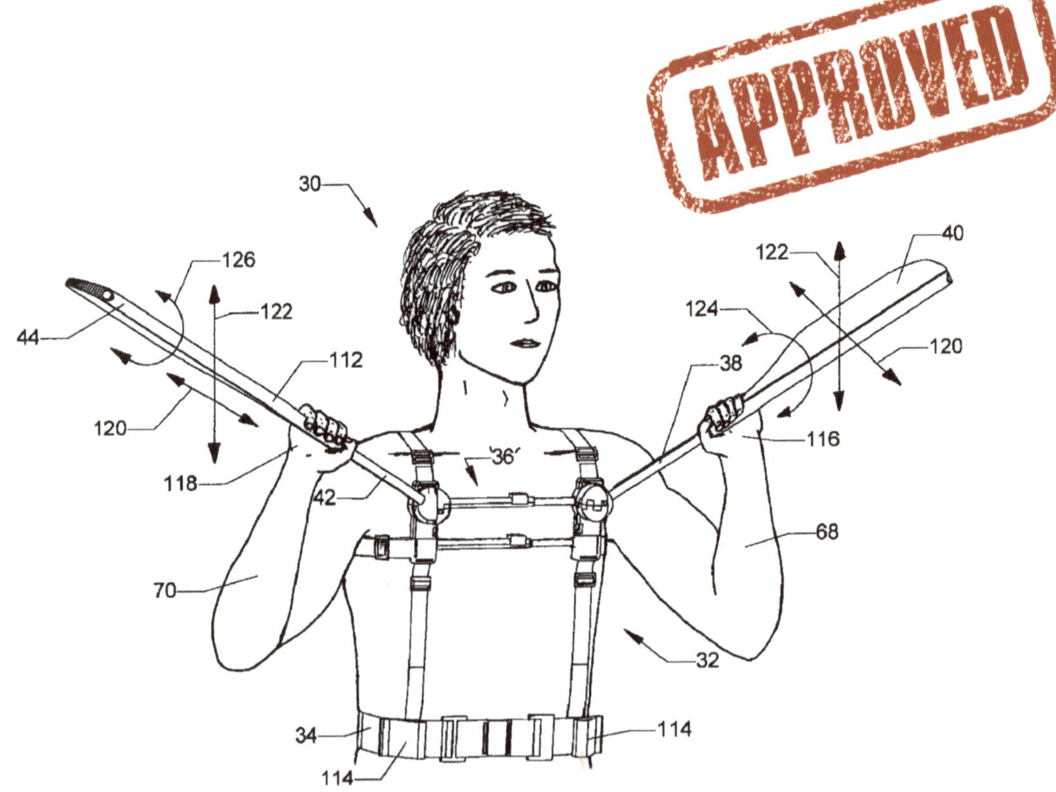

Buttock Kicking Machine

Armstrong, Joe W., *User-Operated Amusement Apparatus for Kicking the User's Buttocks,* UNITED STATES PATENT Patent No. 6,293,874 Bl, Sep. 25, 2001.

An amusement apparatus including a user-operated and controlled apparatus for self-infliction of repetitive blows to the user's buttocks by a plurality of elongated arms bearing flexible extensions that rotate under the user's control. The elongated arms are propelled by the user's movement of the crank, which is operatively connected by a drive train to the central axis of the rotating arms. As the user rotates the crank, the user's buttocks are paddled by flexible shoes located on each outboard end of the elongated arms to provide amusement to the user and viewers of the paddling.

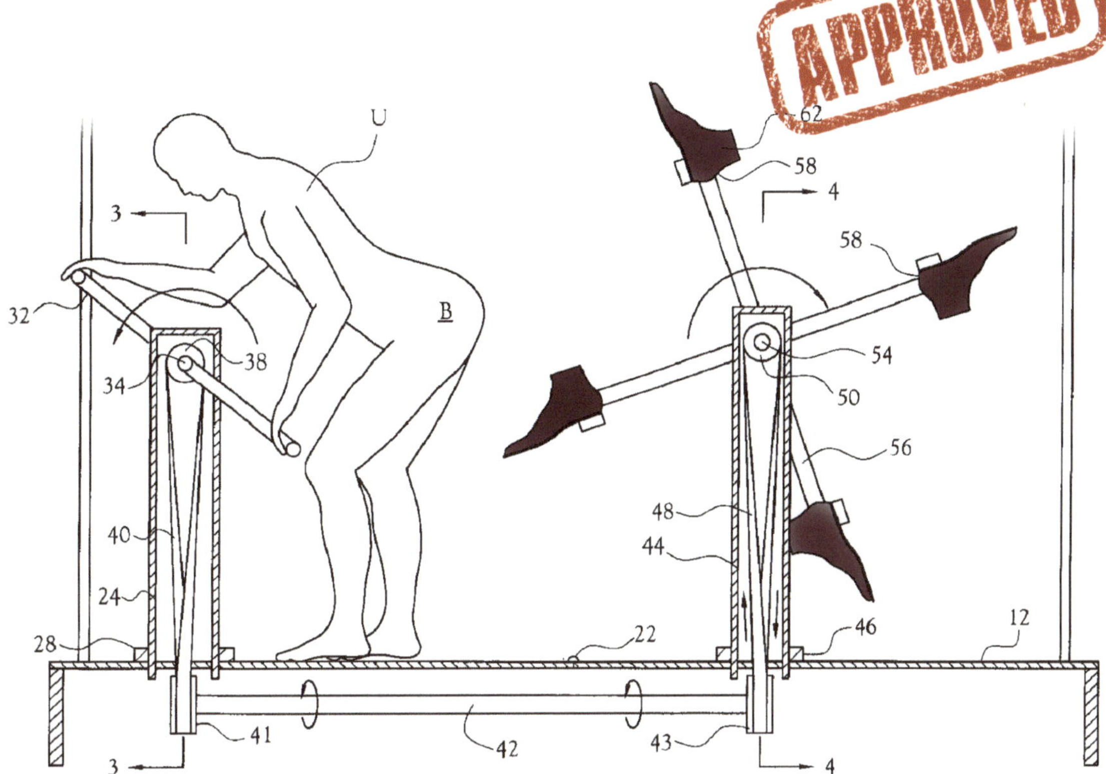

Flatulence Deodorizer

Conant, Brian J., Conant, Myra M., *Flatulence Deodorizer*, UNITED STATES PATENT Patent No. 6,313,371 B1, Nov. 6, 2001.

The present invention relates generally to intestinal discharge control products and, more specifically, to flatulence deodorizers. There are various devices in this field for dealing with the problems of intestinal discharges with some degree of Success. However, all of them are somewhat cumbersome and/or bulky to use. The present invention, the Flatulence Deodorizer, is the first product for this application to use activated charcoal cloth as a deodorizer because it is So much more effective in removing odor than other known agents and because of its highly efficient filtering action, the thickness of the cloth can be significantly reduced without loosing effectiveness.

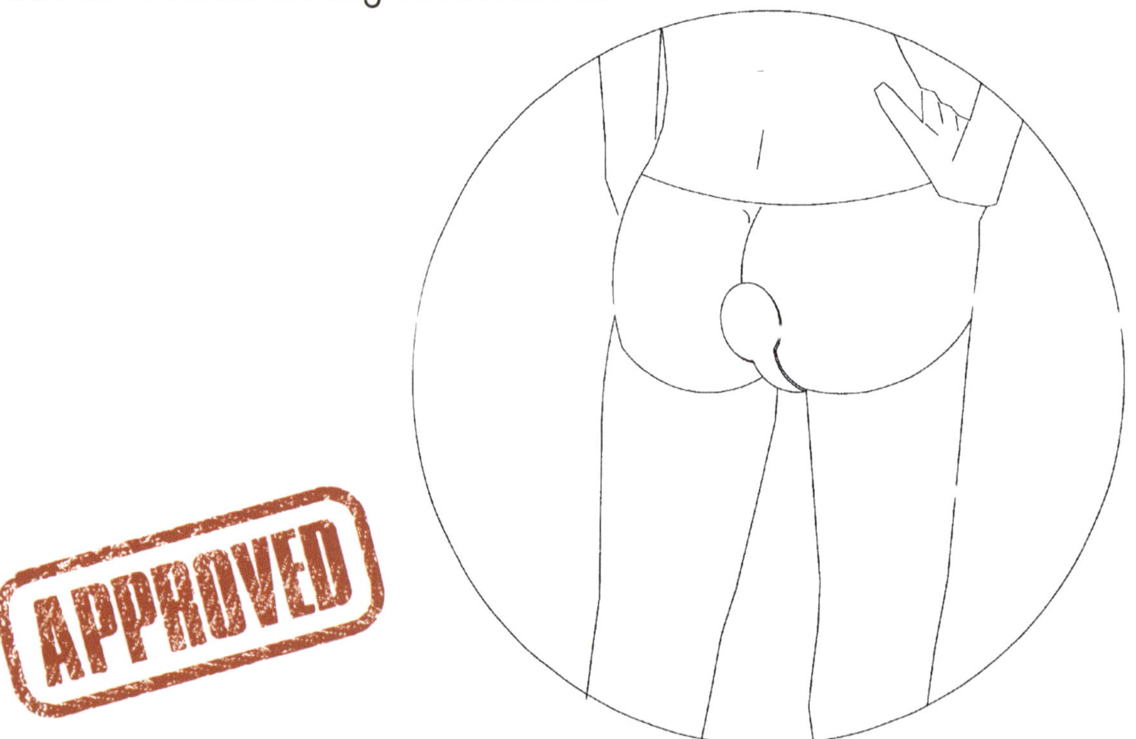

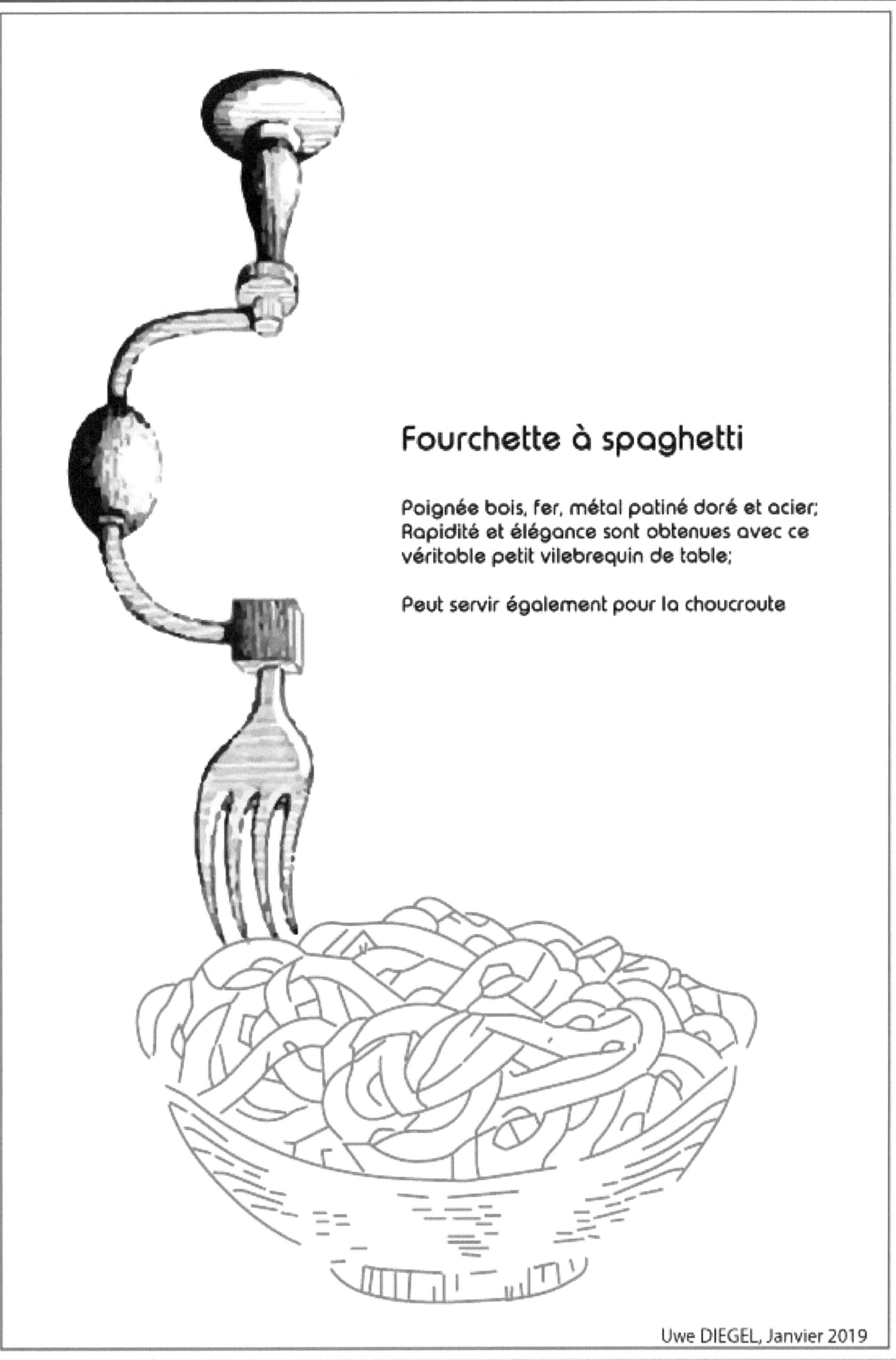

Fourchette à spaghetti

Poignée bois, fer, métal patiné doré et acier;
Rapidité et élégance sont obtenues avec ce
véritable petit vilebrequin de table;

Peut servir également pour la choucroute

Uwe DIEGEL, Janvier 2019

System and Method for Bowling Remotely

Dean. Stiteler, R., *System and Method for Bowling Remotely.* United States patent US20020010032Al, Jan. 24, 2002.

This invention relates generally to the playing of a bowling game by two or more persons not situated at the same physical location. In particular, to a system and method for two or more bowlers to engage in a bowling game at remote sites including a teleconferencing system that allows players located remotely from each other to see, hear, talk, interact and exchange data with each other, an automated bowling scoring system at each bowling site which scores the bowling game at each site at which the game is being played, and interface software transmitting, connecting and combining the bowling sites automated bowling scoring systems through the teleconferencing system. The bowling scoring systems have the capability, by use of the interface software through the teleconferencing system, to transmit the image of their site's bowler's frame-by-frame scorecard, to all remote sites, so that all bowlers can see all score cards on a continuous real-time interactive basis, in a combined, organized and coordinated manner, while they participate in the remote bowling game.

System and Method for Bowling Remotely

Dean. Stiteler, R., *System and Method for Bowling Remotely.* United States patent US20020010032Al, Jan. 24, 2002.

ILLUSTRATION

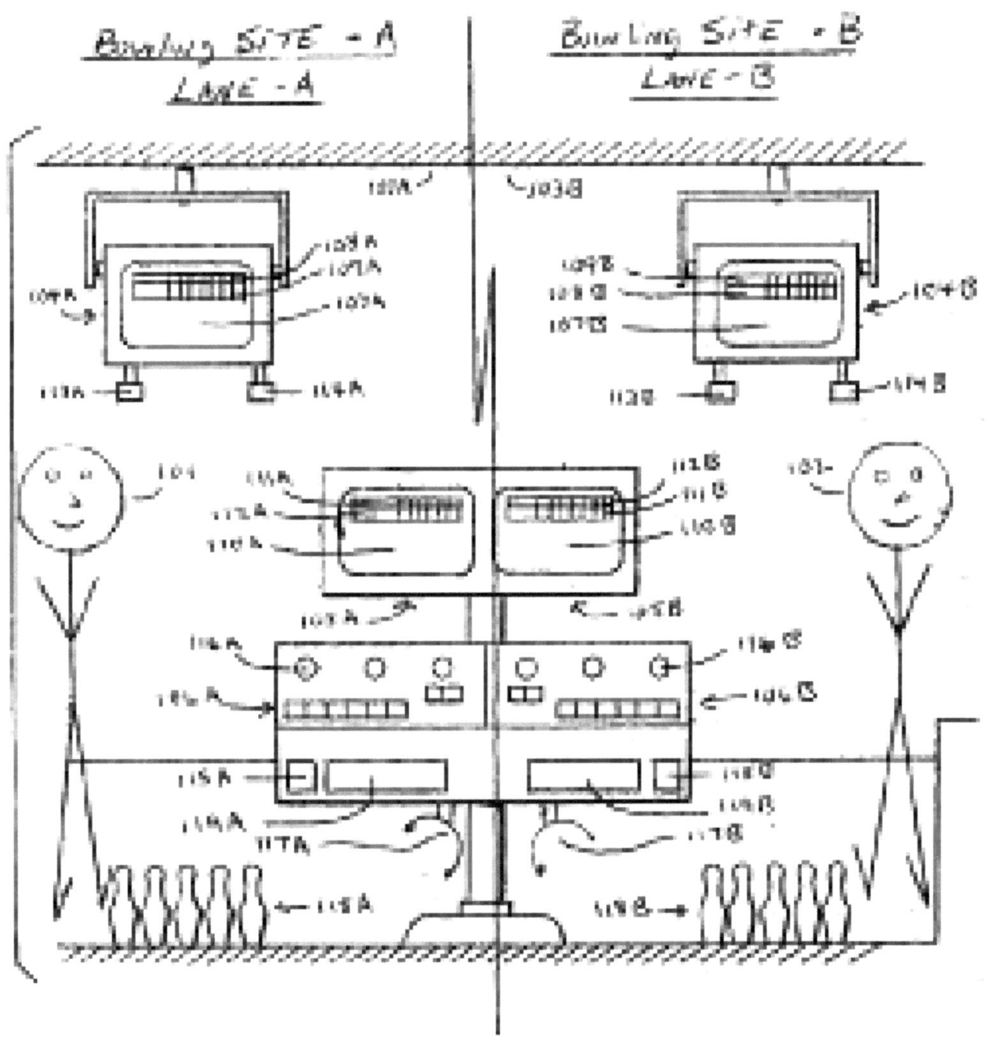

FIG. 1 is an overall illustration of two, physically separate, bowling sites, A and B, with lane configurations arranged in accordance with the present invention's required equipment.

Buttock Support Device

Hart, Karin, *Buttock Support Device,* UNITED STATES PATENT Patent No. 6,360,375 Bl, Mar. 26, 2002.

A Buttocks Support Device is a support device that comprises an abdominal element and a pair ol thigh support elements each of which can be, but is not limited to be, formed as a ring shaped element. Each thigh support element has a buttock section and a midriff or abdominal section, the buttock section being configured to lift and restrain the wearer's buttock. The preferred device includes a sleeve thereover for permitting the "rings" to be tightened without pulling on the wearer's skin. It is a further aspect that the device anchor about the wearer's midriff from below the chest to the widest part ol the hips or at either the waist or the hips, depending upon the wishes ol the wearer.

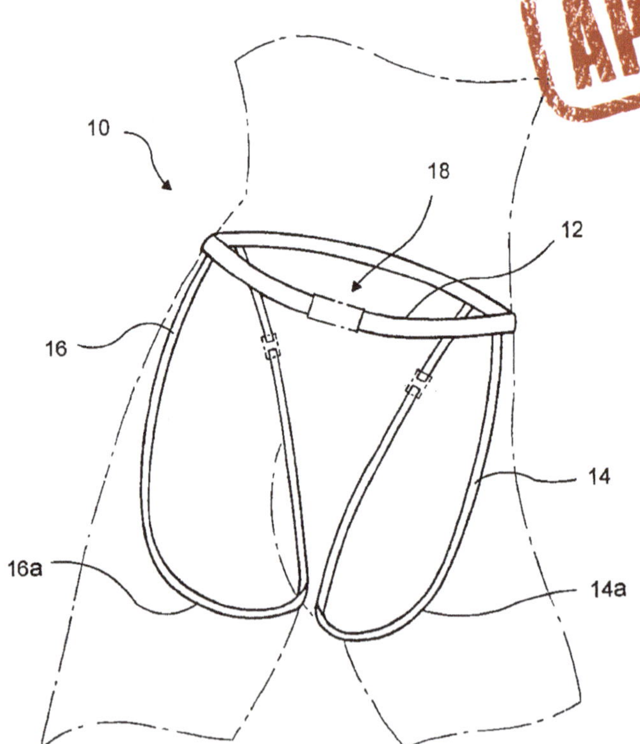

Wobbling Headpiece

Forth, Timothy, *Wobbling Headpiece,* UNITED STATES PATENT Patent No. 6,401,260 Bl, Jun. 11, 2002.

One aspect ol the present invention pertains to a wobbling headpiece that includes a display member having an inner concave portion that substantially surrounds and is substantially disassociated from a head strap. An action mechanism is operably disposed between the display member and the head strap.

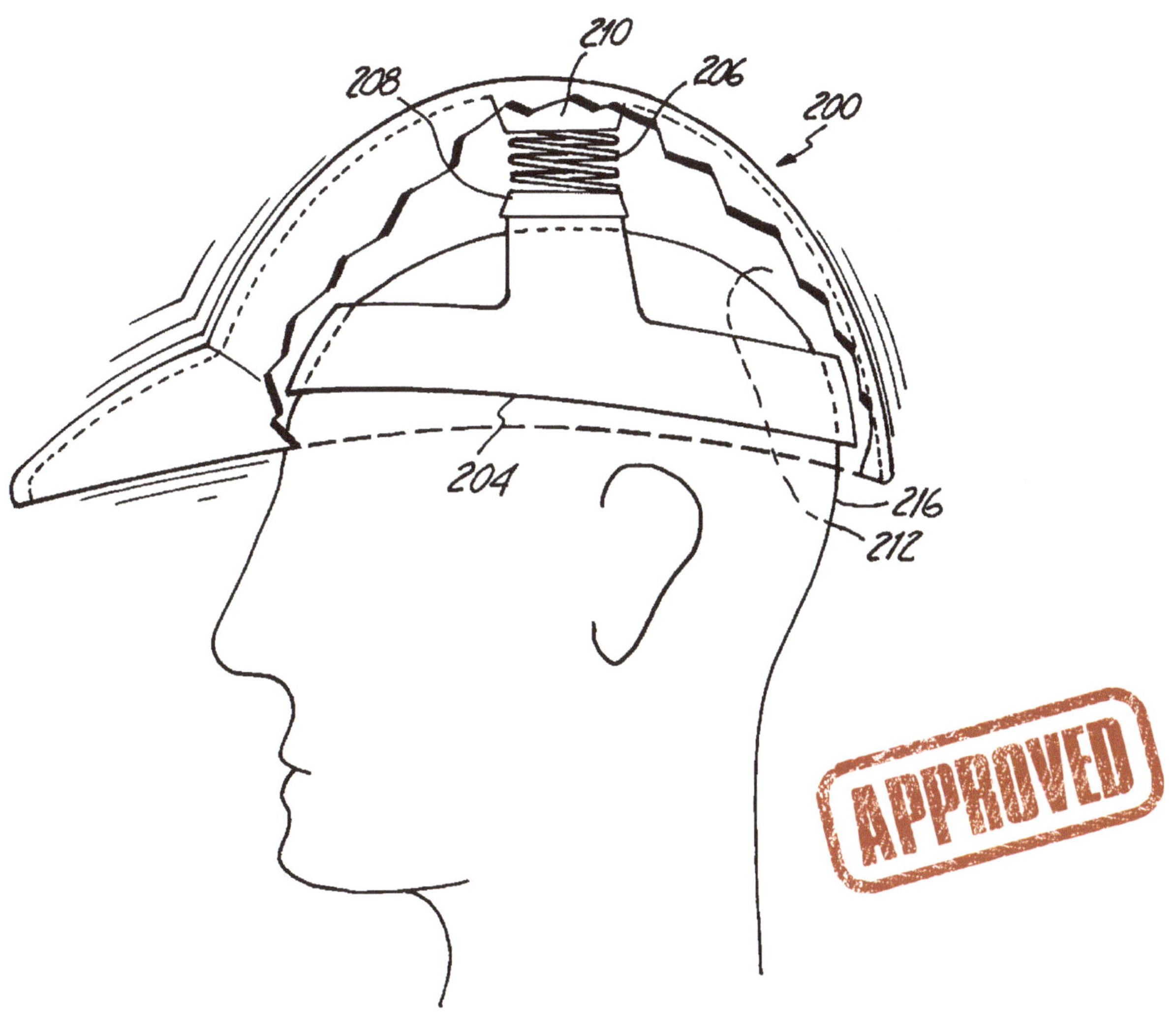

Spaceship with Rotatable Thrust Assembly

Syrovy, George J., Yassini-Fard, Siamak, Yassini-Fard, Rouzbeh, *Passenger Vehicle Employing a Circumferentially Disposed Rotatable Thrust Assembly,* UNITED STATES PATENT Patent No. 6,402,088 Bl, Jun. 11, 2002.

A vertical take-off and landing vehicle that employs a thrust assembly, a fuselage, and an intermediate rotation decoupling interface assembly for rotationally decoupling the thrust assembly from the fuselage. The thrust assembly forms a single combined thrust force about the fuselage in order to form a more stable vehicle during flight.

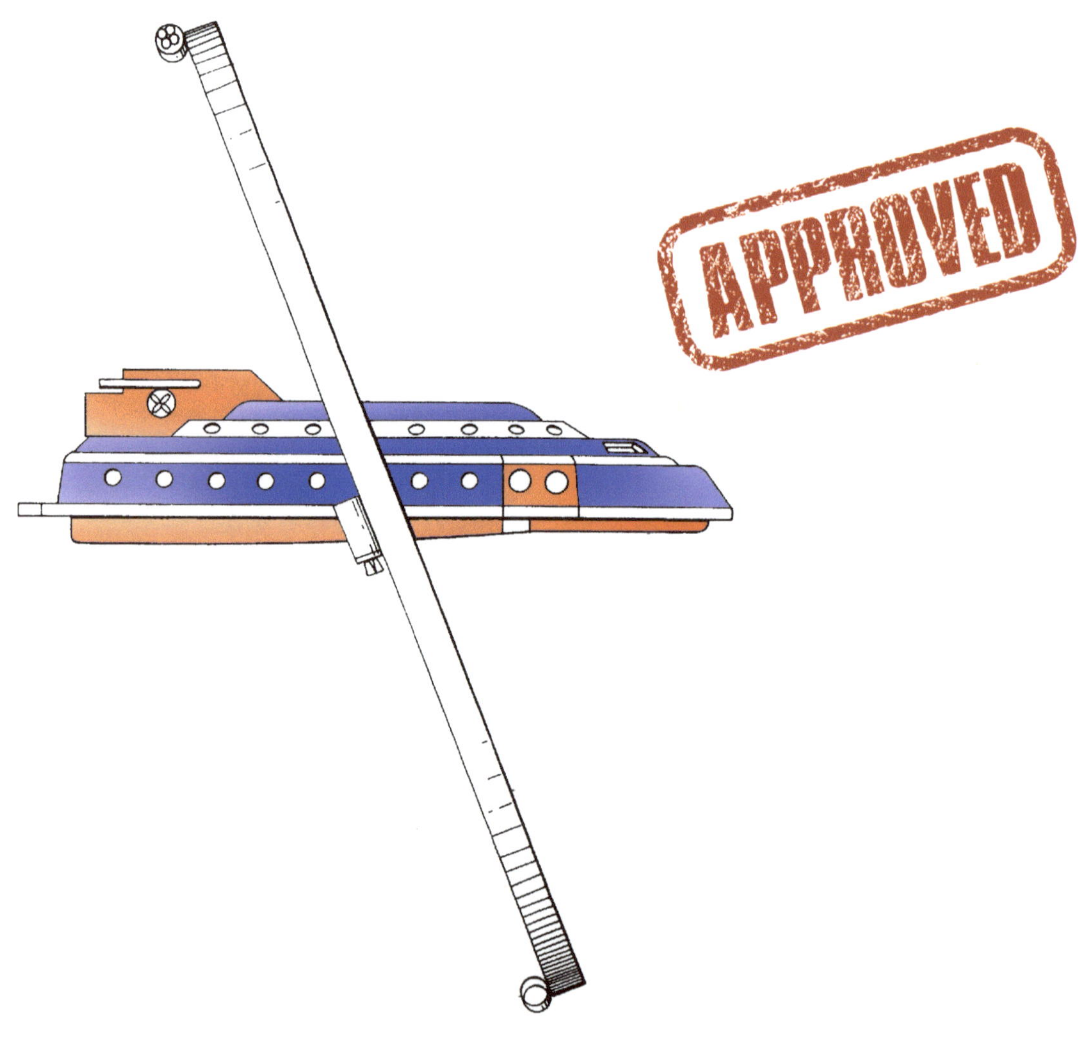

Secure Snake Collar

Boys, Donald Robert Martin, *Collar Apparatus Enabling Secure Handling of a Snake by Tether,* UNITED STATES PATENT Patent No. 6,490,999 Bl, Dec. 10, 2002.

A collar for collaring a snake has an elongated collar sectionforming a physical collar when wrapped around the body portion of the snake. The collar further has a support section for supporting an attachment mechanism for accepting attachment of a tether and a connector system comprising at least two components affixed to strategic portions of the collar section for securing the collar in place around the body portion of the snake. The length of the collar section is such that a portion thereof overlaps itself when fitted around the snake providing an adjustable interface containing separate components of the connector system whereby mating the connector components together, secures the collar in place on the snake. In one embodiment the collar apparatus further includes a concertina movement-neutralization device for reducing concertina movement through the collar.

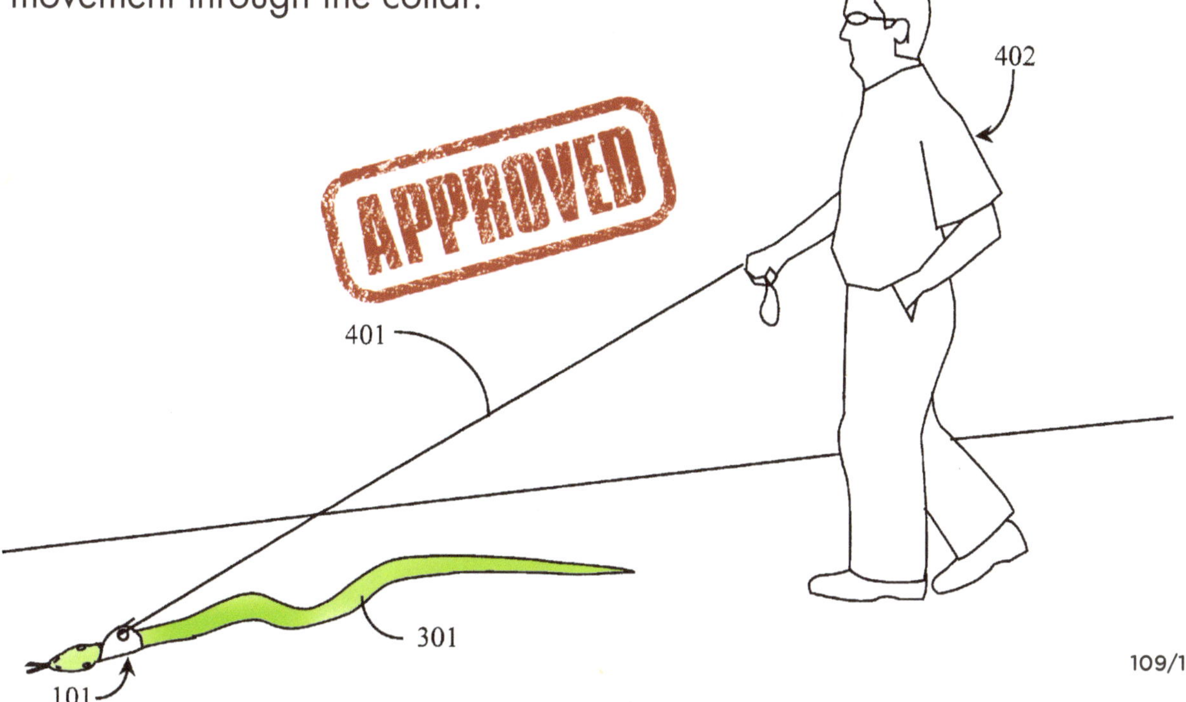

Adjustable Harness and Animal Birth Control Device

Spiller, Karmicheal, *Adjustable Harness and Animal Birth Control Device*, UNITED STATES PATENT Patent No.US 6,647,928 B1, Nov. 18, 2003.

An adjustable harness and animal birth control device for female quadrupeds comprising an adjustable harness having an adjustable waist collar, an adjustable left harness strap, an adjustable central harness strap and an adjustable right harness strap, each of the harness straps being detachably secured to the waist collar, and a birth control device which is detachably secured to the adjustable harness. The adjustable harness utilizes hook and loop fastening means in order to provide proper fitting and adjustment for various sizes of quadrupeds.

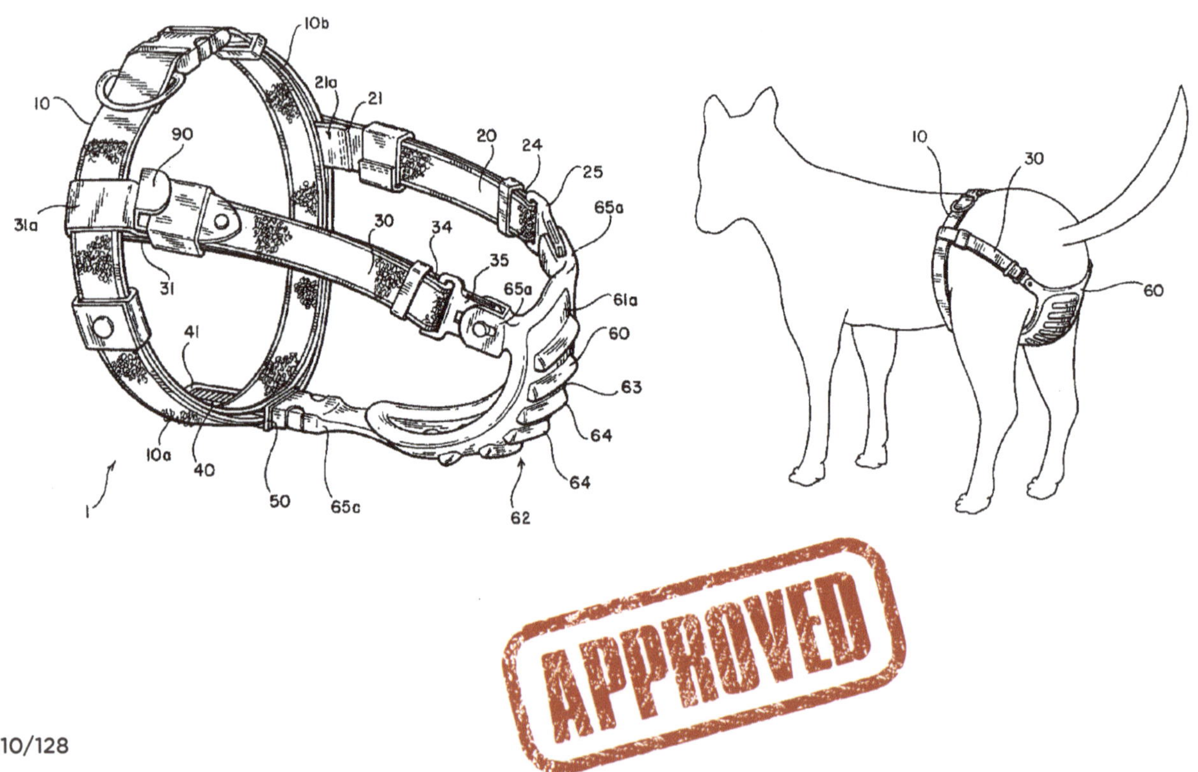

Leaf Gathering Trousers

Kinnier, Paul Frederic, *Leaf Gathering Trousers*, UNITED STATES PATENT Patent No. 6,604,245 B1, Aug. 12, 2003.

A leaf gathering trouser comprised of a pair of flexible leg stalls and a flexible net, said net attached at opposing side edges to cooperating portions of the leg stalls and substantially occupying a space between the leg stalls in order to make contact with loose leaves located upon a ground surface and to accumulate said leaves into a pile for disposal while a user is wearing the leg stalls and walking in a normal manner. The net, comprised of a web section and a solid section, can be permanently attached to the leg stalls or releasably attached thereto by means of cooperating rows of zippers and zipper heads.

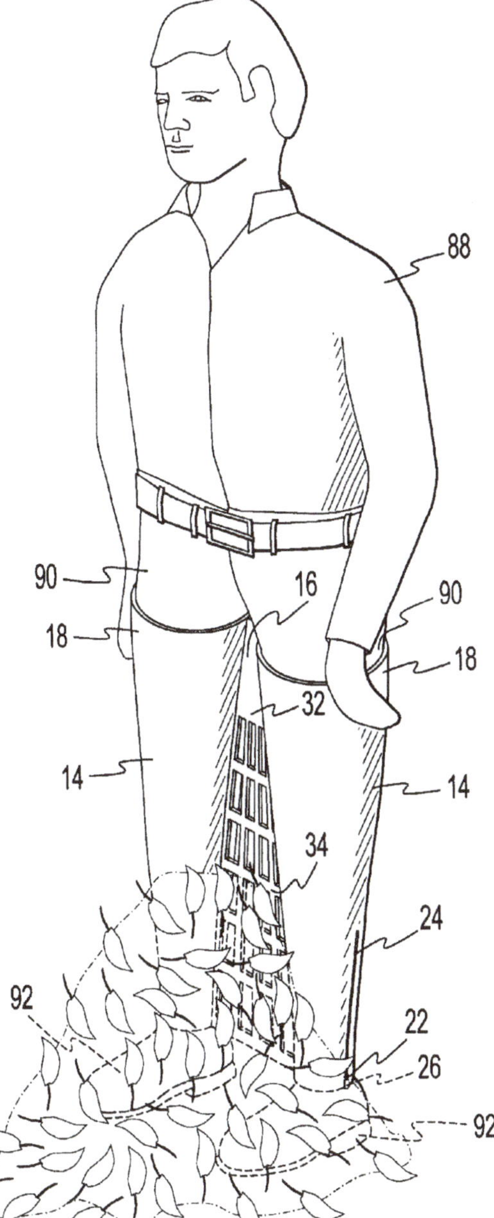

Banana Protective Device

Agulnik, David B., *Banana Protective Device,* UNITED STATES PATENT Patent No. US 6,612,440 B1, Sep. 2, 2003.

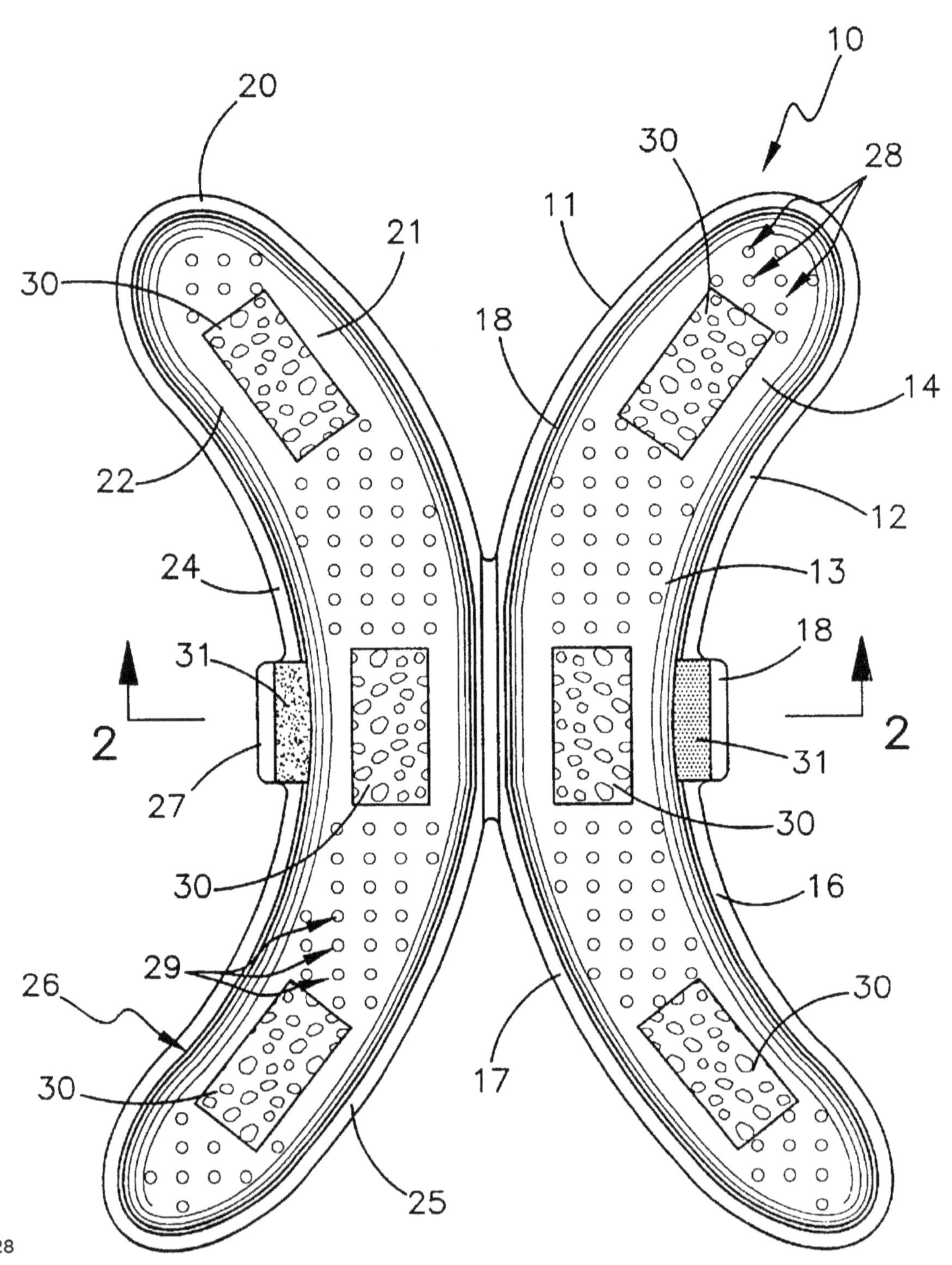

Banana Protective Device

Agulnik, David B., *Banana Protective Device,* UNITED STATES PATENT Patent No.US 6,612,440 B1, Sep. 2, 2003.

A banana protective device for storing and transporting a banana carefully. The banana protective device includes a container having a first cover member and a second cover member being hingedly attached to the first cover member and being adapted to store a banana therein; and also includes pad members being securely disposed upon the first and second cover members for protecting and cushioning the banana; and further includes fastening members being attached to the first and second cover members for fastenably closing the first and second cover members together.

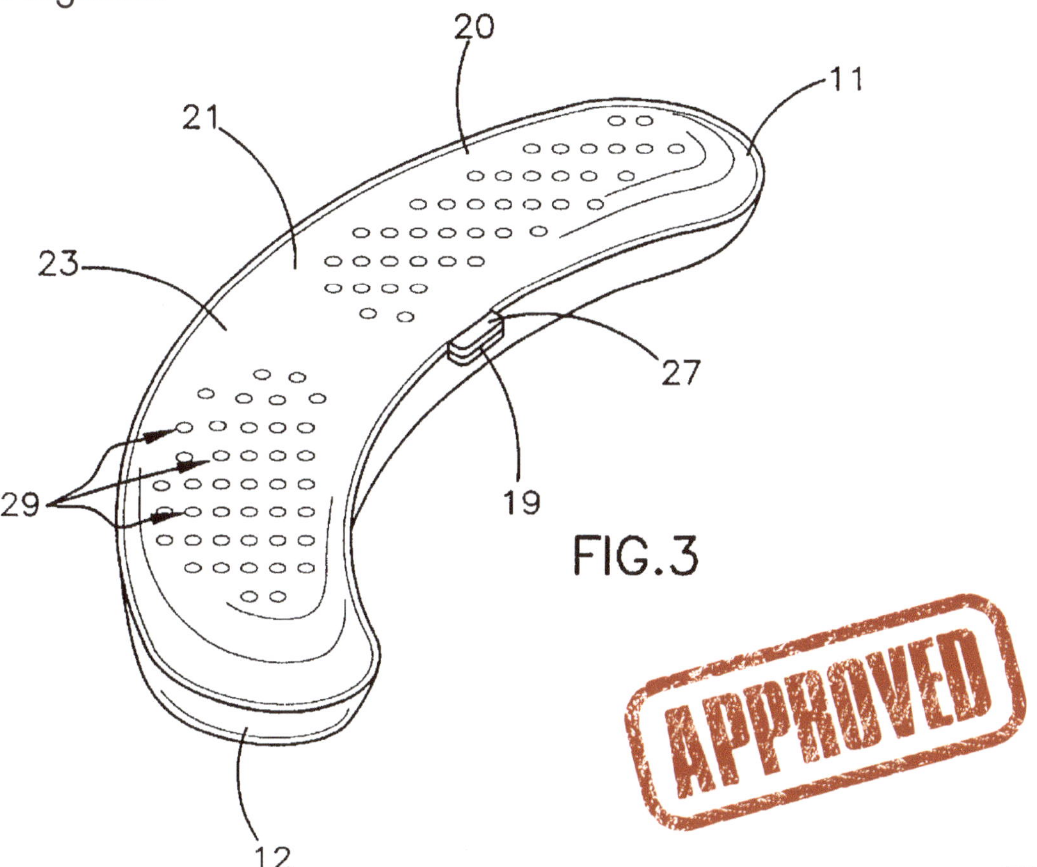

FIG.3

Beerbrella

McMullin, Mason Schott, Bell, Robert Piatt, See, Mark Andrew, *Beerbrella*, UNITED STATES PATENT Patent No. 6,637,447 B2, Oct. 28,2003.

The present invention provides a small umbrella ("Beerbrella") which may be removably attached to a beverage container in order to shade the beverage container from the direct rays ol the sun. The apparatus comprises a small umbrella approximately five to seven inches in diameter, although other appropriate sizes may be used within the spirit and scope ol the present invention. Suitable advertising and/or logos may be applied to the umbrella surface for promotional purposes. The umbrella may be attached to the beverage container by any one ol a number of means, including clip, strap, cup, loam insulator, or as a coaster or the like. The umbrella shaft may be provided with a pivot to allow the umbrella to be suitably angled to shield the sun or for aesthetic purposes.

Forehead Support Apparatus

Page, Eric D., *Forehead Support Apparatus,* UNITED STATES PATENT Patent No.US 6,681,419 B1, Jan. 27, 2004.

A forehead support apparatus for resting a standing users forehead against a wall above a bathroom commode or urinal or beneath a showerhead. The apparatus includes a mounting member adapted for attachment to an upright bathroom wall either above the commode or urinal or below the showerhead.

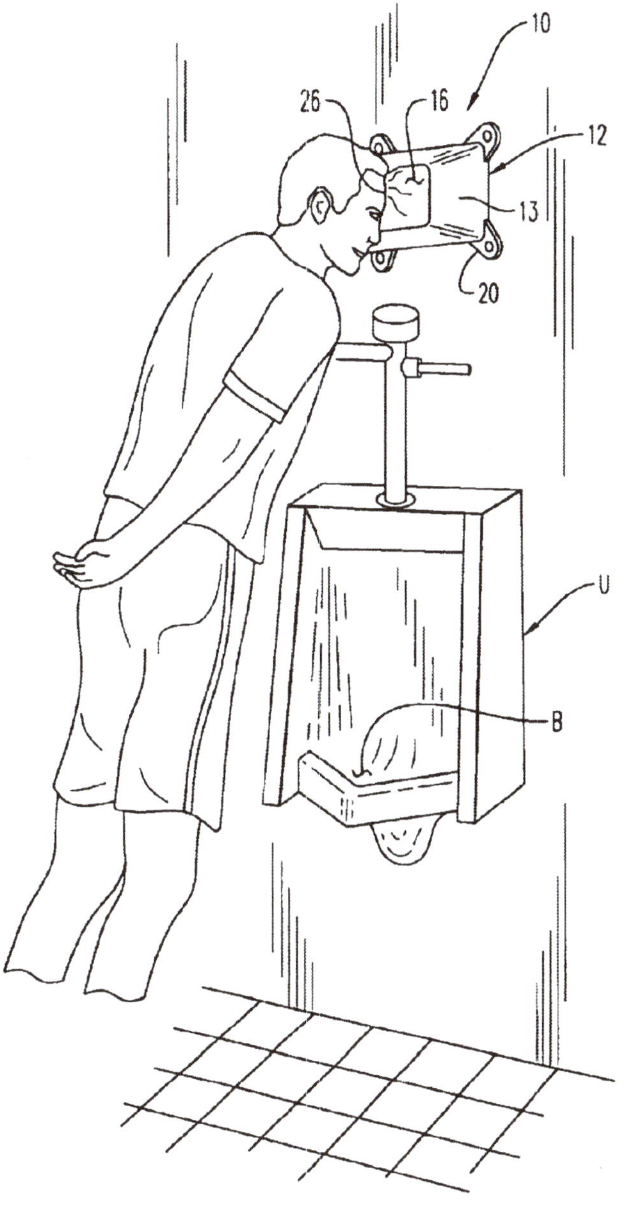

Dog Bark Translator

Suzuki, Mutsumi, *Apparatus for Determining Dog's Emotions By Voval Analysis of Barking Sounds and Method for the Same*, UNITED STATES PATENT Patent No. US 6,761,131 B2, Jul. 13,2004.

A method of determining a dog's emotions from its voice. The invention follows the procedures of converting dog's voices into electrical audio signals, extracting characteristics in a time to frequency component relation map of the audio signals as a input voice pattern, storing in advance in memory reference voice patterns for various emotions that respectively represent characteristics of time to frequency component relation maps, comparing the input voice pattern with the reference voice patterns, and determining what a dog feels by declaring emotion of the particular reference voice pattern.

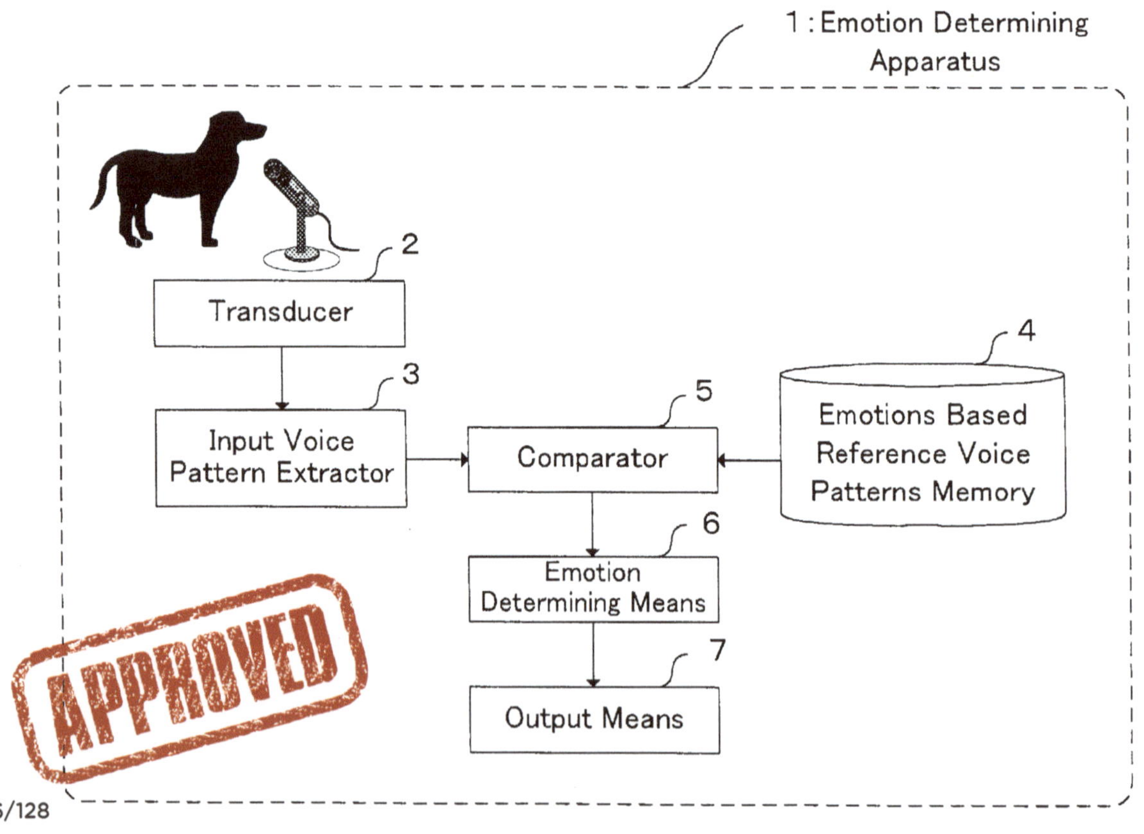

Dolphin Fin Swimming Accessory

Otto, Clifton S., *Dolphin Fin Swimming Accessory*, UNITED STATES DESIGN PATENT Patent No. US D494,652 S, August 17, 2004.

The dolphin fin swimming accessory is intended to be worn while swimming with dolphins in the wild, to assist the swimmer with imitating the underwater maneuvers of the dolphins.

The broken lines showing a human figure are for illustrative purposes only and do not form part of the claimed design.

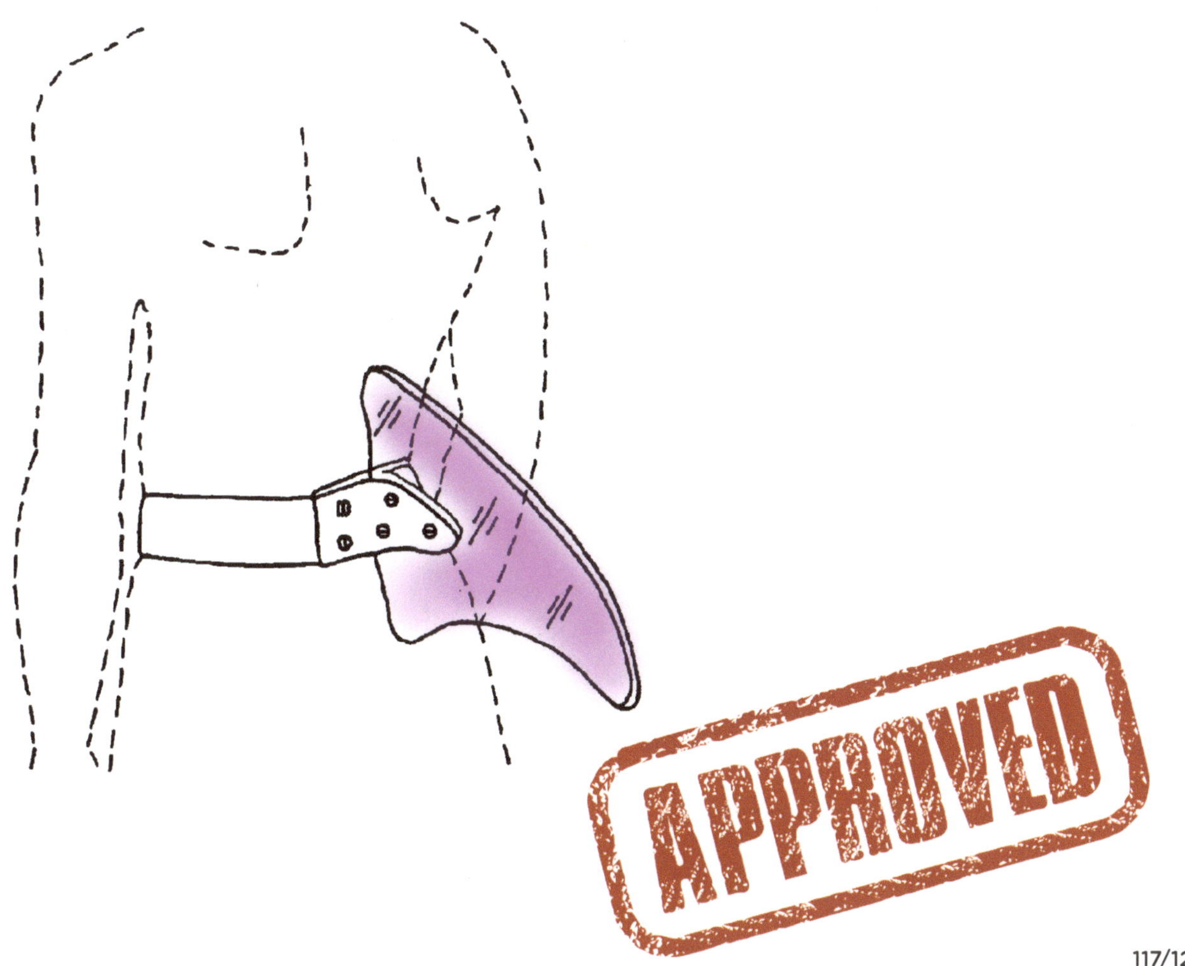

TV Mute Finger Ring

Murray, William P. Jr., *TV Mute Finger Ring*, UNITED STATES PATENT Patent No. 6,778,380 B2, Aug. 17,2004.

TV Mute Finger Ring with a hollow C shaped finger ring housing. The housing contains the standard electronics and IR transmitting LED associated with activating the mute function of a standard TV. The housing also contains a battery type electrical power source. The IR transmitter is covered by a transparent plastic lens that is flush with the outer surface of said C shaped housing. The plastic lens is positioned so that said lens and said IR transmitting LED are pointed outwardly in the general direction of said TV.

Light Bulb Changer

Magdi, Thomas, *Light Bulb Changer*, UNITED STATES PATENT Patent No. US 6,826,983 Bl, Dec. 7,2004.

A light bulb changer method and apparatus that contains components that allows for instantly detecting a burned out light, automatically removing the burned out light, and automatically replacing the burned out light with a replacement bulb. The changer operates without human intervention, and can be assembled from a kit having a light fixture, detecting sensor, removing and replacement hardware. The kit can allow a consumer to assemble the changer for use as a novelty item, and/or also to be used as a working light fixture, such as a table lamp, and the like. The changer can also be used as a retrofit for existing light fixtures so that the existing light fixtures can be modified.

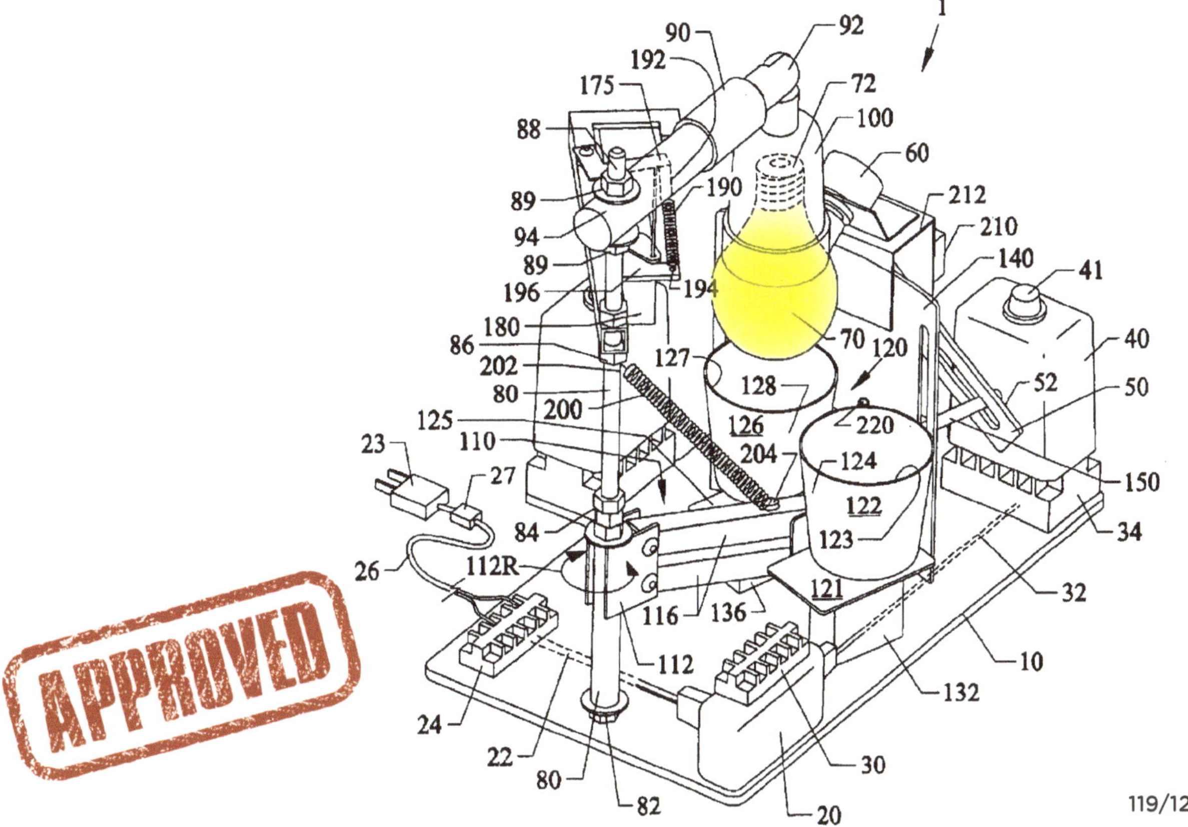

Gun-Shaped Insect Swatter

Conte, Francis Luca, *Insect Swatter*, UNITED STATES PATENT Patent No. 6,851,218 BI, Feb. 8,2005.

An insect swatter includes an elongate rod with an elastic lash fixedly joined to a distal end thereof. The lash is sized for being stretched from the rod distal end to adjacent a proximal end of the rod so that release of the lash results in spontaneous contraction thereof for swatting the insect. In an exemplary embodiment, the swatter is in the form of a pistol, with the lash extending from the distal end of the rod to a latch operated by a trigger. Aiming the rod toward the insect and pulling the trigger releases the lash for swatting the insect.

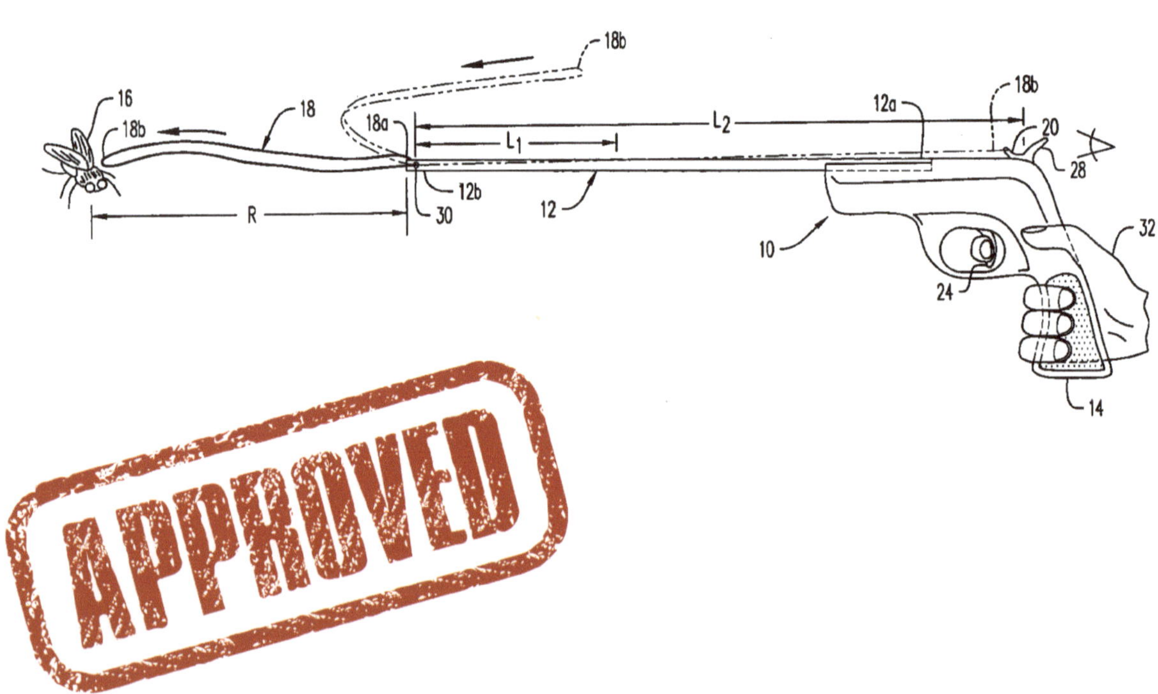

Vibrating, Body-Piercing Jewelry

Andrews, John T., Whittinghill, Kenneth R., *Vibrating, Body-Piercing Jewelry* , UNITED STATES PATENT Patent No. 6,865,907 B2, Mar. 15, 2005.

A vibrating, body-piercing jewelry item having a vibrating motor unit, a housing for the vibrating motor unit, a post, a keeper, retainer or clamping device for holding the item on a wearer's body, a power source for operating the vibrating motor unit, and an actuator for the vibrating motor unit. The vibrating, body-piercing jewelry may be worn on a part of the body that is either unpierced or pierced.

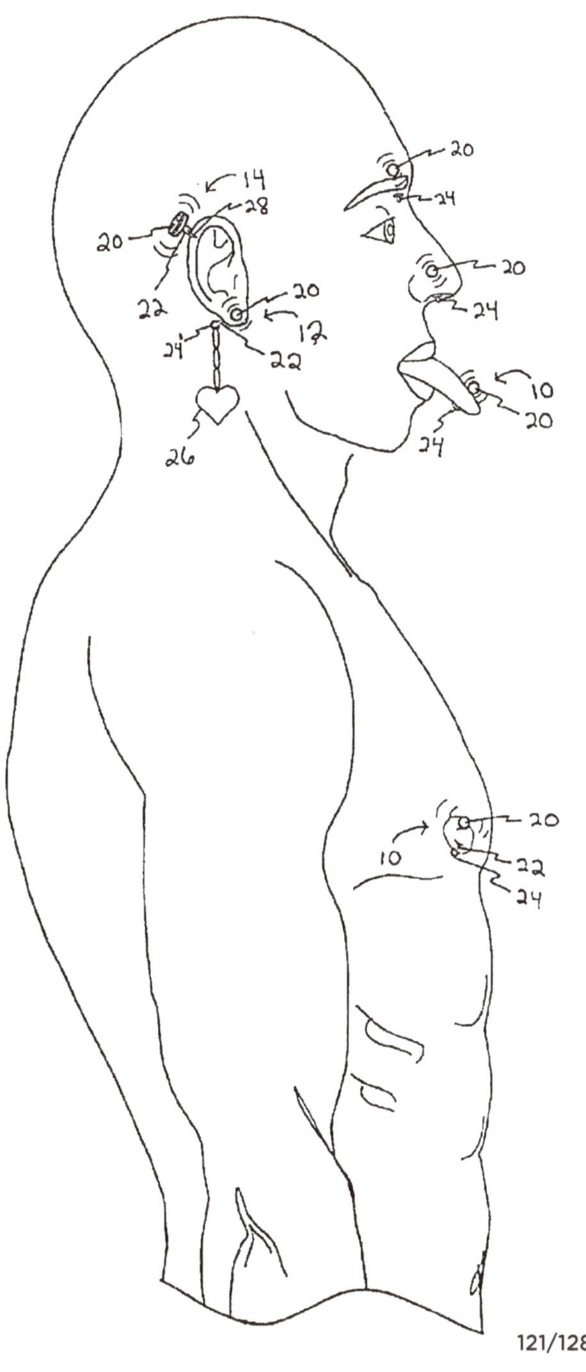

Edible Garments

Brink, Jeffrey H., *Garments Having Edible Components and Method for Making Same*, UNITED STATES PATENT Patent No.6,872,119 B2, Mar. 29,2005.

A garment having edible components associated therewith can be made by stringing apertured edible items or candies onto fabric portions, for example, waistbands of panties, bikinis, etc. Strings of fabric can accommodate a variety of different types of edible materials and such materials can be of many shapes and sizes, in particular can reflect any particular holiday event in the year (e.g., hearts for Valentine's Day; shamrocks for St. Patrick's Day; pumpkins for Halloween, etc.). The garments can be re-used with or without rethreading edible items or candies of choice, and a kit for facilitating this practice forms one aspect of the present invention.

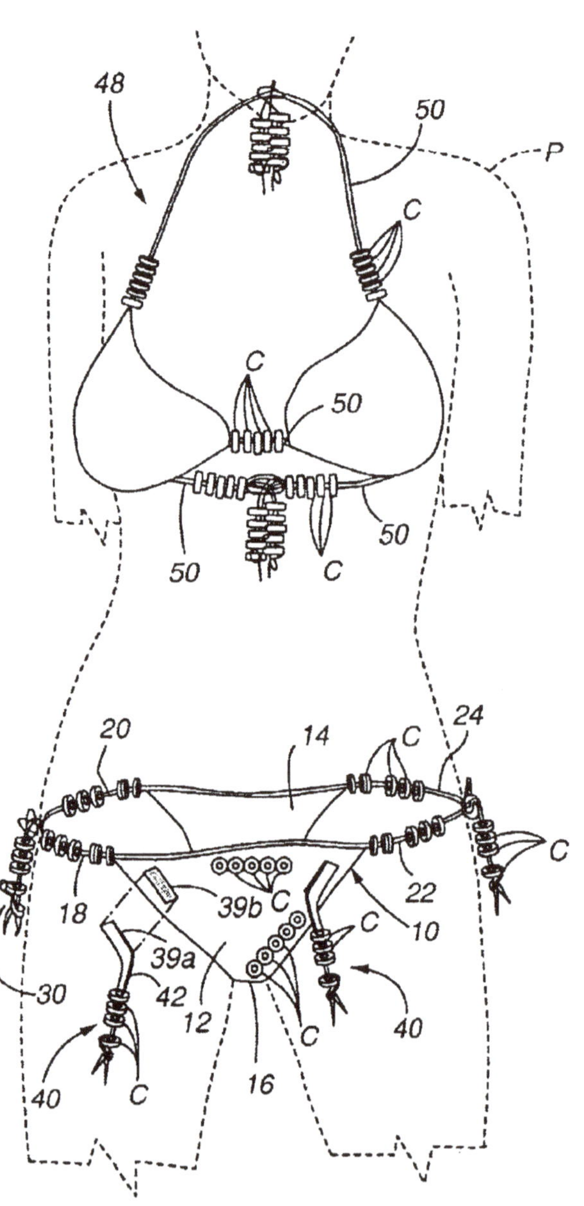

Combination Powered Parachute and Motorcycle

Bragg, Albert J., *Combination Powered Parachute and Motorcycle*, UNITED STATES PATENT Patent No. 6,877,690 Bl, Apr. 12,2005.

A combination powered parachute and motorcycle modifies an initially conventional motorcycle with the addition of various flight components to provide sustained flight for the machine. A peripheral and overhead safety structure is installed upon the motorcycle, with a second flight engine, propeller, folding propeller guard, and fuel system also installed. The flight engine and all of its systems are completely independent of the conventional motorcycle engine used for surface propulsion. A set of laterally disposed stabilizer wheels is also provided for transition from ground to flight and from flight to ground operation. Lift is provided by a folding parafoil device of either the ram air inflated or partially pneumatically inflated type.

Manually Self-Operated Butt-Kicking Machine

Leavitt, J. Reese, *Manually Self-Operated Butt-Kicking Machine*, UNITED STATES PATENT Patent No.S 2006/0094518, May 4,2006.

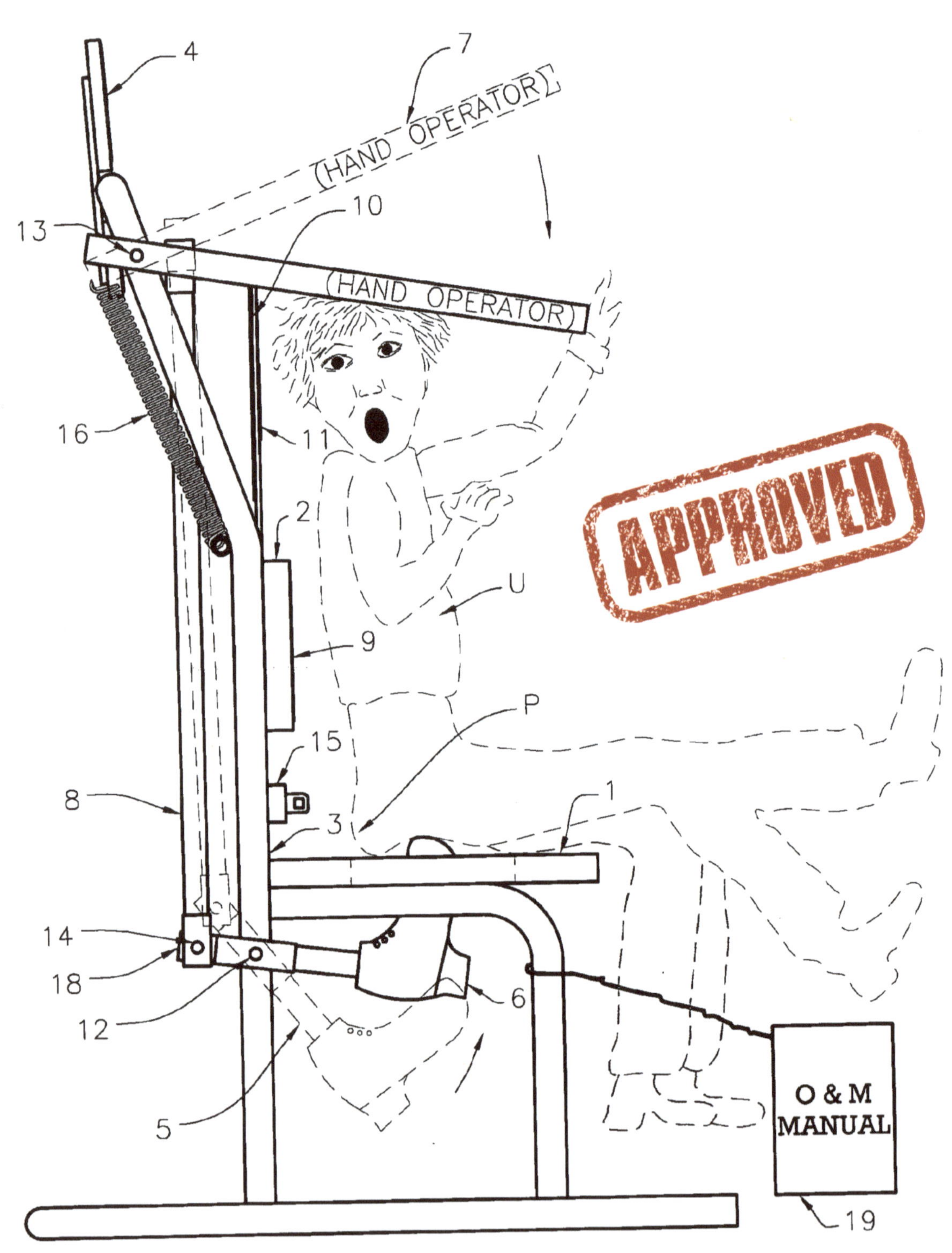

Manually Self-Operated Butt-Kicking Machine

Leavitt, J. Reese, *Manually Self-Operated Butt-Kicking Machine,* UNITED STATES PATENT Patent No.S 2006/0094518, May 4,2006.

The Manually Self-Operated Butt-Kicking Machine is in the form of a chair with a hole in the bench. The user sits on the bench with his posterior centered over the hole. A seatbelt holds the user in place. There is a kicking mechanism located below the hole, which has a boot attached to it. When the user or operator pulls the hand-operated lever, the boot kicks the users' posterior through the hole in the bench. The Butt kicker is very user friendly with the number of kicking repetitions, type of repetitions, speed of operation, amplitude or height of the kicking cycle, magnitude of the kicking force, and impact and energy of the kick all controlled by the user or operator. This invention is a new, novel, and unique machine with multiple uses, which range from amusement to fundraising and from motivation to discipline. The objectives of this invention are also many, including, but not limited to, teambuilding, self-therapy, to inspire creativity, and to be used as a model for future devices and works of art.

"World famous"
MANUALLY SELF-OPERATED BUTT-KICKING MACHINE
"For your butt-kicking enjoyment"

OPERATING INSTRUCTIONS

1. Sit firmly on seat.
2. Attach seat belt for your protection and commitment.
3. Reach up and grab hand operator.
4. Move hand operator up and down as required to activate.
5. Apply butt kicking as necessary until desired result is achieved.
6. Enjoy !

Methane Emissions Recycler

Herrema, Markus Donald, *Process for the Utilization of Ruminant Animal Methane Emissions,* UNITED STATES PATENT Patent No. 6,982,161 Bl, Jan. 3, 2006.

A process for the utilization of the methane contained within ruminant animal exhalation, specifically to a process that utilizes the methane contained within ruminant animal exhalation as a source of carbon and/or energy for the production of methane-utilizing microorganisms in a microorganism growth-and-harvest apparatus.

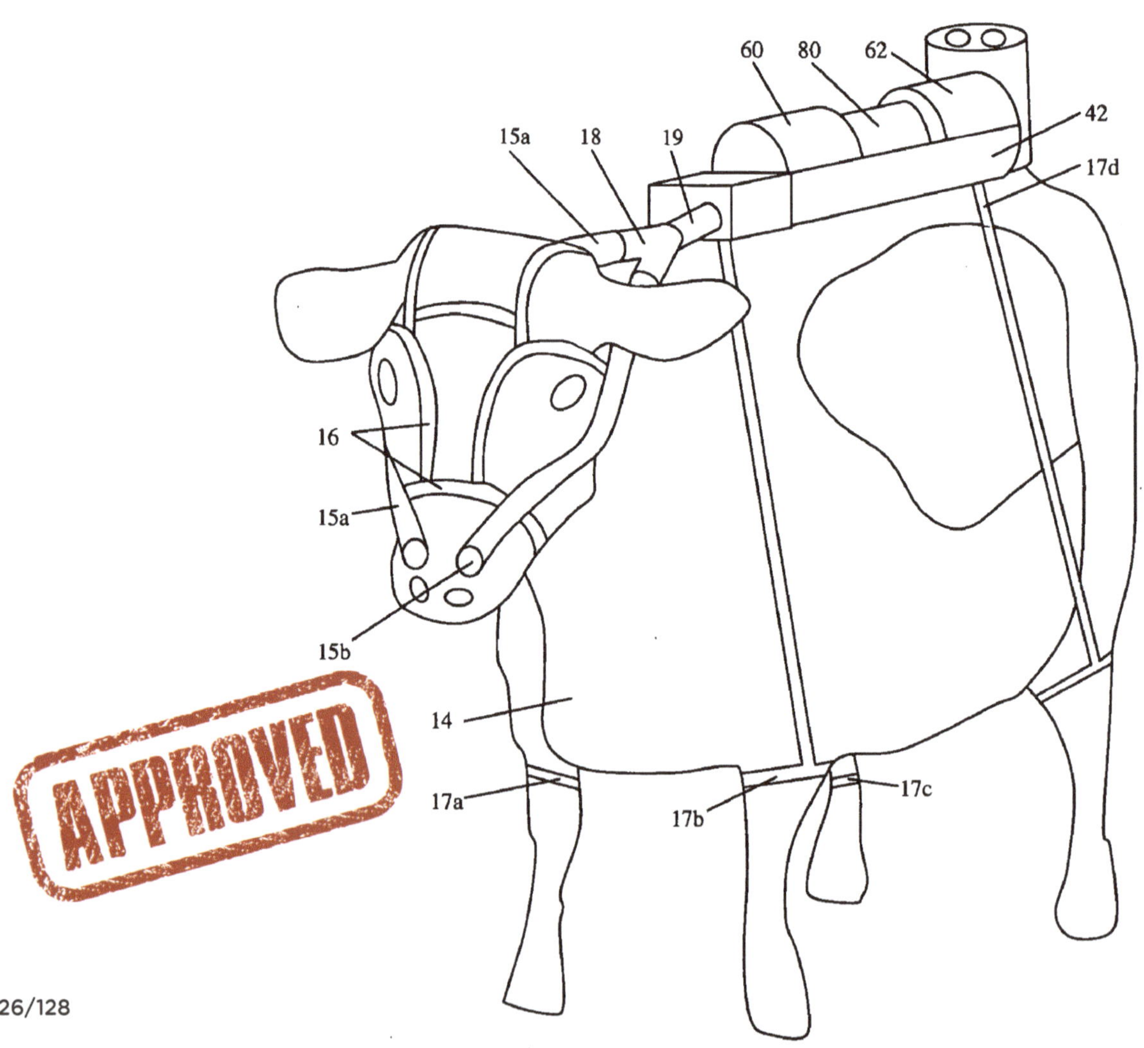

Exercise Kit for Personal Flotation Device

Kolarick, Robert, Kolarick, Jacquelin, *Exercise Kit for Personal Flotation Device*, UNITED STATES PATENT Patent No. 2008/0124991 Al, May 29,2008.

The instant invention relates to a kit for converting an elongated flexible noodle-type personal floatation device into a floating exercise assembly. Specifically, the rider straddles the flexible noodle-type device while rotating the first exercising assembly and/or the second exercising assembly for exercising the user's lower and upper body, respectively.

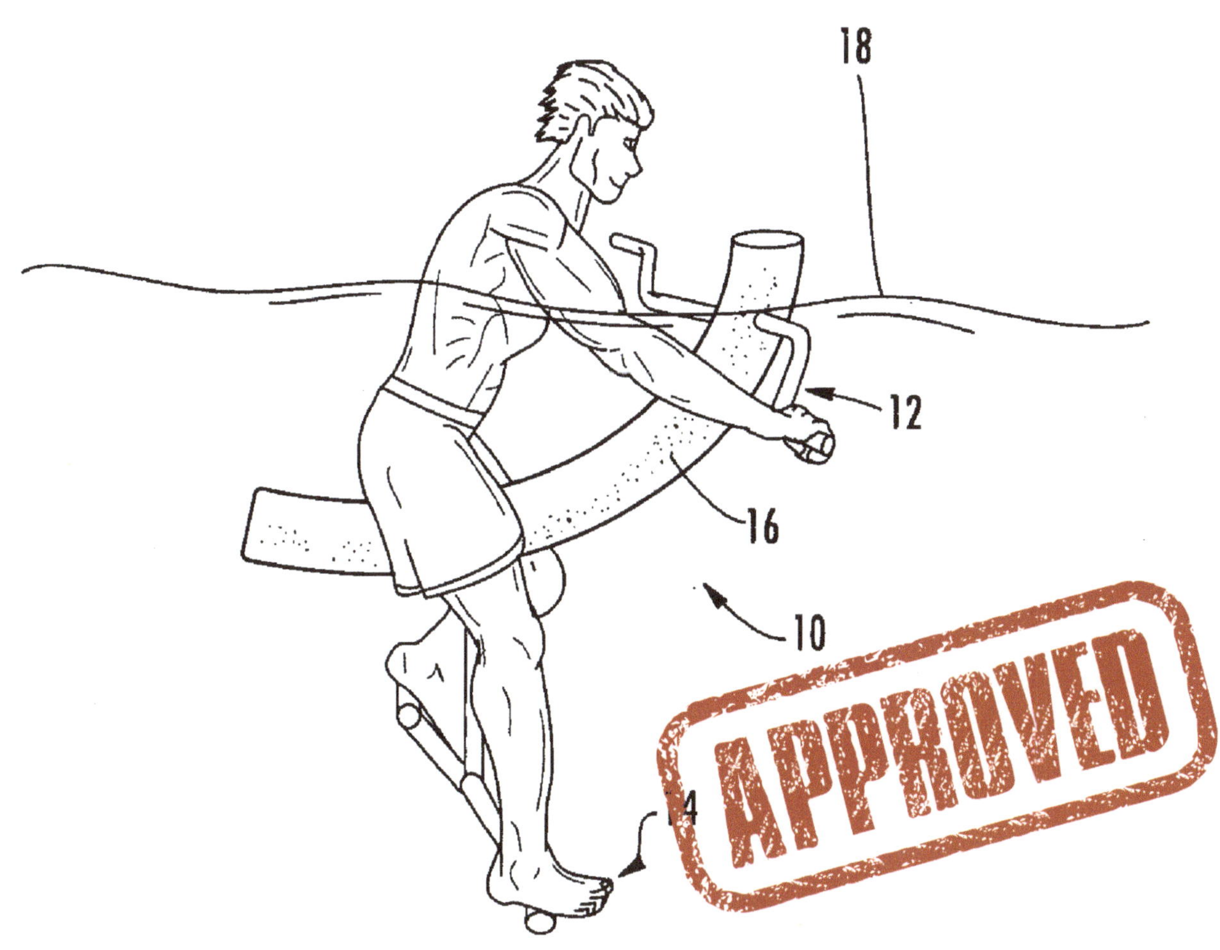